Also by Jalal Toufic

Two or Three Things I'm Dying to Tell You (Post-Apollo, 2005)

Undying Love, or Love Dies (Post-Apollo, 2002)

Forthcoming (Atelos, 2000)

Over-Sensitivity (Sun & Moon, 1996)

(Vampires): An Uneasy Essay on the Undead in Film (Station Hill, 1993; revised and expanded ed., Post-Apollo, 2003)

Distracted (Station Hill, 1991; 2nd ed., Tuumba, 2003)

'Âshûrâ': This Blood Spilled in My Veins

Toufic, Jalal.
'Âshûrâ': This Blood Spilled in My Veins / Jalal Toufic.
Includes bibliographical references.
ISBN 9953-0-0460-9

Copyright © 2005 by Jalal Toufic
All rights reserved

'Âshûrâ': This Blood Spilled in My Veins has been made possible in part by the Islamic World Arts Initiative, generously supported by the Doris Duke Foundation for Islamic Art and administered by the Lower Manhattan Cultural Council.

With the exception of the six film stills from Dreyer's *The Passion of Joan of Arc* on page 56, with regards to all the book's photographs © by Jalal Toufic.

The Arabic calligraphy of the title on the cover is by Samîr al-Sâyigh

Design: Hatem Imam and Jalal Toufic

Printed by Calligraph Printing & Trading, Lebanon

'Âshûrâ': This Blood Spilled in My Veins

Jalal Toufic

Forthcoming Books

Acknowledgments

"'Âshûrâ'; or, Torturous Memory as a Condition of Possibility of an Unconditional Promise" was published in *Home Works: A Forum on Cultural Practices in the Region: Egypt, Iran, Iraq, Lebanon, Palestine and Syria*, compiled by Christine Tohme and Mona Abu Rayyan (Beirut, Lebanon: the Lebanese Association for Plastic Arts Ashkal Alwan, 2003), pp. 94-101. A shorter, untitled version of it ends my book *Undying Love, or Love Dies* (Post-Apollo, 2002).

The author thanks Gilbert Hage.

Table of Contents

'Âshûrâ'; or, Torturous Memory as a Condition of Possibility of an Unconditional Promise — 9

This Blood Spilled in My Veins — 19

Martyrs — 57

Posthumous Martyrs — 71

Notes — 89

'Âshûrâ'; or, Torturous Memory as a Condition of Possibility of an Unconditional Promise

Can one still give and maintain millenarian promises in the twenty first century? But first, a more basic question: can one still promise at all?

Al-Husayn, the grandson of the prophet Muhammad and the son of the first Shi'ite imâm, 'Alî b. Abî Tâlib, was slaughtered alongside many members of his family in the desert in 680. This memory is torture to me.

"I am not allowed to weep, because I'll become blind were I to do so," says old Victoria Rizqallah at the end of my video *'Âshûrâ': This Blood Spilled in My Veins*, 2002. But wouldn't losing the ability to weep be even more detrimental and sadder than going blind? I would prefer to (be able to) weep even were I to go blind as a result of that—to weep over going blind? Isn't that better than becoming inhuman? "For others too can see, or sleep, / But only human eyes can weep" (Andrew Marvell, "Eyes and Tears").

But, basically, one can say *this memory is torture to me* of every memory, since each reminiscence envelops at some level the memory of the origin of memory, the torture that had to be inflicted on humans in order for them to be able to remember. If we feel a tinge of pain, a pang, when we remember it is not necessarily because the past vanishes, is no more (Einstein's relativity and Dōgen's Zen tell us otherwise in two different ways),[1] but because each memory reactivates in us however faintly the genealogy of the establishment of memory. In Twelver Shi'ites' yearly ten-day commemoration 'Âshûrâ', we witness a condition of possibility of memory, in a Nietzschian sense.

"To breed an animal *with the right to make promises*—is not this the paradoxical task that nature has set itself in the case of man? is it not the real problem regarding man?

"That this problem has been solved to a large extent must seem all the more remarkable to anyone who appreciates the strength of the opposing force, that of *forgetfulness*. Forgetting is no mere *vis inertiae* as the superficial imagine; it is rather an active and in the strictest sense positive faculty of repression…[2]

"Now this animal which needs to be forgetful, in which forgetting represents a force, a form of *robust* health, has bred in itself an opposing faculty, a memory, with the aid of which forgetfulness is abrogated in certain cases—namely in those cases where promises are made…

"'How can one create a memory for the human animal? How can one impress something upon this partly obtuse, partly flighty mind, attuned only to the passing moment, in such a way that it will stay there?'

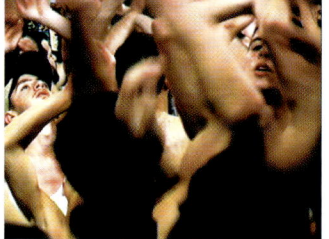

"One can well believe that the answers and methods for solving this primeval problem were not precisely gentle; perhaps indeed there was nothing more fearful and uncanny in the whole prehistory of man than his *mnemotechnics*. 'If something is to stay in memory it must be burned in: only that which never ceases to *hurt* stays in the memory'[3]—this is a main clause of the oldest (unhappily also the most enduring) psychology on earth.[4] One might even say that wherever on earth solemnity, seriousness, mystery, and gloomy coloring still distinguish the life of man and a people, something of the terror that formerly attended all promises, pledges and vows on earth is *still effective*... Man could never do without blood, torture, and sacrifices when he felt the need to create a memory for himself; the most dreadful sacrifices and pledges (sacrifices of the first-born among them),[5] the most repulsive mutilations (castration, for example),[6] the cruelest rites of all the religious cults (and all religions are at the deepest level systems of cruelties)—all this has its origin in the instinct that realized that pain is the most powerful aid to mnemonics.

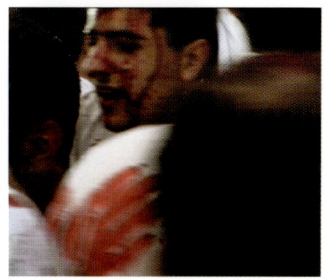

"If we place ourselves at the end of this tremendous process, where the tree at last brings forth fruit, where society and the morality of custom at last reveal *what* they have simply been the means to, then we discover that the ripest fruit is the *sovereign individual*, like only to himself, liberated again from morality of customs, autonomous and supramoral (for 'autonomous' and 'moral' are mutually exclusive), in short, the man who has his own independent, protracted will and the *right to make promises*... And just as he is bound to honor his peers, the strong and reliable (those with the *right* to make promises)—that is, all those who promise like sovereigns, reluctantly, rarely, slowly, who are chary of trusting, whose trust is a mark of *distinction*, who give their word[7] as something that can be relied on because they know themselves strong enough to maintain it in the face of accidents, even 'in the face of fate'—he is bound to reserve… a rod for the liar who breaks his word even at the moment he utters it.

"… Ah, reason, seriousness, mastery over the affects, the whole somber thing called reflection, all these prerogatives and showpieces of man: how dearly they have been bought! How much blood and cruelty lie at the bottom of all 'good things'!"[8]

The preservation of the events of 'Âshûrâ' takes place at two levels: in *'âlam al-mithâl* (The World of the Archetypal Images), aka *'âlam al-khayâl* (The World of the Imagination),[9] where they are, in a transfigured version, eternal, outside the corrosive, dimming sway of chronological time, as well as the labyrinthine temporality of the realm of undeath, where al-Husayn would run the risk of forgetting who he is, of forgetting himself; and in historical time, through the bodily and emotional tortures endured during the yearly ten-day commemorative ceremony,[10] which are the means to breed in the human being,[11] a forgetful creature ("And verily We made a covenant of old with Adam, but he forgot, and We found no constancy in him" [Qur'ân 20:115]), a historical memory. But the memory that the ceremony of 'Âshûrâ' is trying to maintain is not only or mainly that of the past, but the memory of the future, that of the promise of the coming of the Mahdî, the Shi'ite messiah, as well as the corresponding promise of Twelver Shi'ites to wait for him. The exemplary promise has until now been the messianic one, for at least three reasons. First, it has been the longest lasting, spanning centuries, even millennia. Second, it has been maintained "in the face of accidents, even 'in the face of fate' ": Twelver Shi'ites have maintained the promise to wait for the successor of al-Hasan al-'Askarî, the eleventh imâm, who died in 260 AH/873-74, even though the latter apparently left no son, and even though the occultation of the presumed twelfth imâm has by now persisted for over a millennium; and they have maintained their expectation that the twelfth imâm will fulfill his promise to appear again. Third, it implicates a supramoral, antinomian attitude. Hence Sabbatai Zevi's "strange actions," which included causing ten Israelites to eat "fat of the kidney" in 1658, an act that is strictly prohibited by the Torah and punishable by *excision* (getting cut off from among one's people); reciting the following benediction over the ritually forbidden fat: "Blessed are Thou, O Lord, who permittest that which is forbidden"; and abolishing the fast of the Seventeenth of Tammuz in 1665. Hence also the Qarmatîs' sacking and desecration of the Ka'ba in 930 and then their abolishing of the Sharî'a during the Zakariyya al-Isfahânî episode in Ahsâ'. And hence the Nizârîs' abolishing of the Sharî'a starting with the proclamation by Hasan *'ala dhikrihi'l-salâm* (on his mention be peace) of the Great Resurrection in Alamût in 8 August 1164 from a pulpit facing west, a direction opposite to the Ka'ba in Mecca, the direction toward which all Moslems have to turn during their prayer.[12] The basic and ultimate promise is to wait for the messiah, who, truly sovereign, supramoral, will initially break the Law, including the "laws" of nature[13] (indeed his miraculous coming notwithstanding his death or millennial occultation is often announced by supernatural events "such as the rise of the sun from the west, and the occurrence of the solar and lunar eclipses in the middle and the end of the month of Ramadan, respectively, against the natural order of such phenomena"[14]), then, upon establishing redemption, altogether abolish the Law, which applies only to the unredeemed world, thus allowing his initiates to be resurrected into a lawless world.[15] The ceremony of 'Âshûrâ' is the flip side of the belief in the promise of the hidden imâm. I would thus wager that the introduction of the ceremonies of 'Âshûrâ' and of Ta'ziya coincided with a period when Twelver Shi'ism was not on the rise but, on the contrary, when the continued belief in the coming of the Mahdî was in danger of extinction. From this perspective, the condemnation of these ceremonies by many Twelver Shi'ite 'ulamâ'[16] is either shortsighted or else implies that they would like to fully supplant the Mahdî. Were 'Âshûrâ' to be discontinued across the Twelver Shi'ite community, then sooner or later the memory of the promise of the occulted imâm would fade away. The basic reason the ceremony's participants hit themselves and self-flagellate[17] is not some unreasonable feeling of guilt for not succoring imâm Husayn and his family around 1300 years ago, but that such cruelty is a most efficient mnemonic. Some may object that the morality of mores, etc., has already born fruit, namely the one who can promise on the basis of his ability to remember, and that therefore there is no longer any need for such a cruel mnemonic. This would be the case for promises of normal spans (but not for one that spans millennia),[18] and were we not reaching a point where the immemorial process, described by Nietzsche, by which humans succeeded to a large extent to create a memory for themselves is beginning to be reversed. As Jean-Joseph Goux points out: "Every society has produced, exchanged, and consumed, but it is only in the modern era in the West that the economy has been separated from all religious, political, and moral ends in order to constitute a system ruled by its own laws, which are those of market exchange.... the exchange destroys the bond produced as it proceeds. The equivalent exchange is without memory and without obligation. It is a relation that cancels and neutralizes itself at the moment of its fulfillment."[19] And Paul Virilio, the thinker of dromology, writes: "*The acceleration of real time*, the limit-acceleration of the speed of light, not only dispels geophysical extension (…) but, first and foremost, it dispels the importance of the *longues durées* of the local time of regions, countries and the old, deeply territorialized nations. (…) Past, present and future—that tripartite division of the time continuum—then cedes primacy to the immediacy of a tele-presence… This is (…) the time of light and its speed—a *cosmological constant* capable of conditioning human history."[20] We started with a flighty mind attuned only to the passing moment; then we had a torturous process of thousands of years of pain and sacrifices to inculcate in humans a memory, and consequently a deep time; but we have now reached someone who is being conditioned by the hegemony of market exchange over all other ends, and programmed by telecommunications at the speed of light, for example TV (on average in the USA, children aged 2 to 11 watch about 23 hours of TV per week, and teenagers watch about 22 hours per week),[21] to hear and see a live "event" anywhere in the world of globalization only to instantly forget about it: Rwanda, then sports, then a commercial for a soap brand, etc.; and to restrict his or her interaction with others to an economic transaction, "which by its symmetry and instantaneous reciprocity… is without fidelity or commitment, an abstract relation that exhausts the disaffected mutuality it implies, without leaving any trace."[22] In order to describe the human being at the beginning of the twenty first century in front of his TV, we can instead of resorting to Virilio's contemporary terms revert to the terms Nietzsche was using to describe man in prehistory: "partly obtuse, partly flighty mind, attuned only to the passing moment." We (or more precisely the West) will more and more be able to accurately predict through computer simulation,[23] but we (or more precisely the West) will less and less be able to give promises.

23 March 2002
Jalal Toufic, Beirut
jtoufic@cyberia.net.lb

Betty, Paris:
As for the book you volunteered to give me as a gift and promised to send to me, Italo Calvino's *Invisible Cities*,

one of the lines in the first edition of my first book, *Distracted*, says: "My apology turned out to be unnecessary, for he had already forgiven my age": isn't youth the age when one gives so many promises—including to oneself—that remain unfulfilled—at least for a long time? Promising is one of those actions that seem to be the easiest—after all, it is a performative (see J.L. Austin's *How to Do Things with Words*)—when actually it is the most difficult since unnatural: "To breed an animal *with the right to make promises*—is not this the paradoxical task that nature has set itself in the case of man?" (Nietzsche).
Best
Jalal

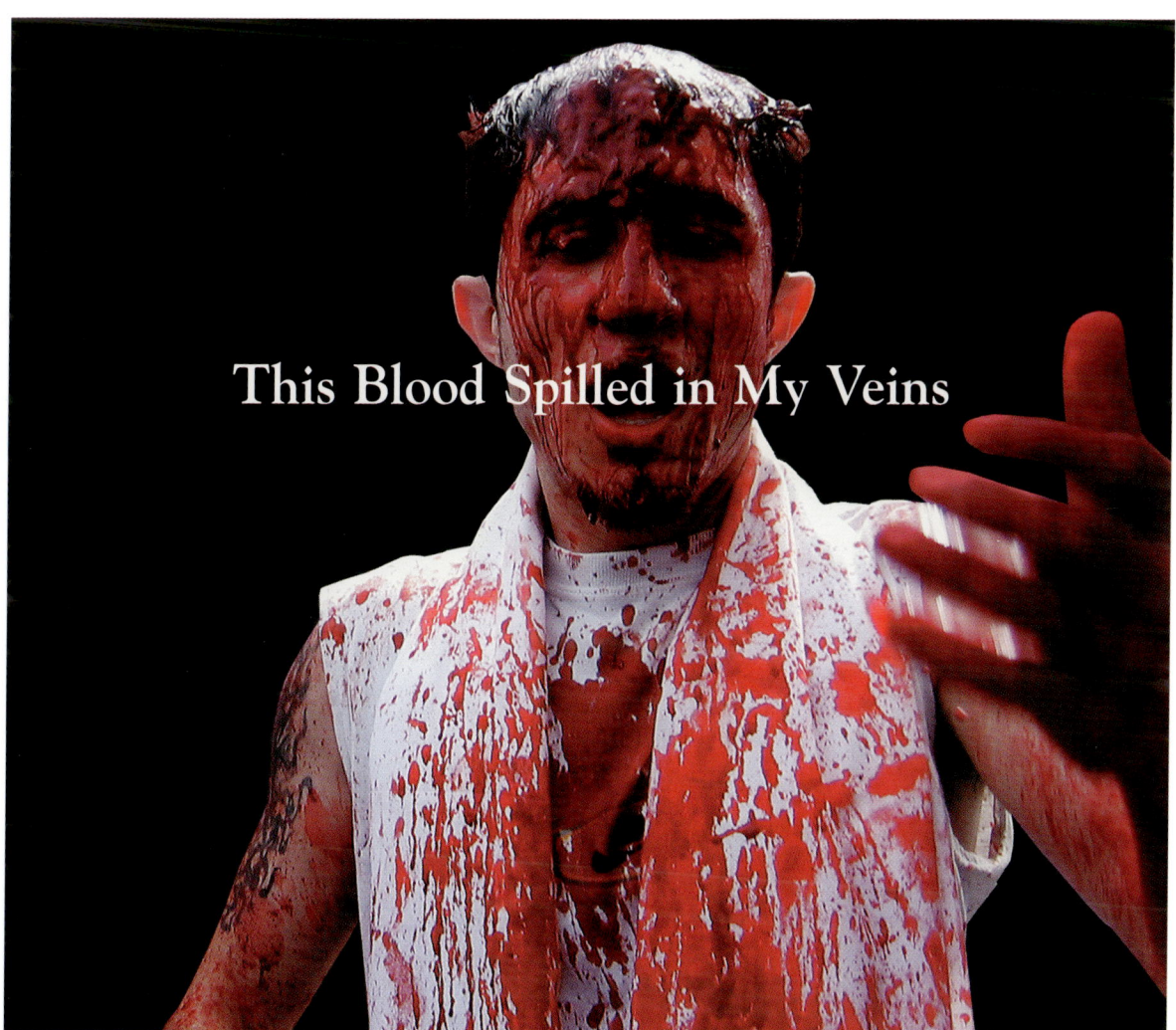

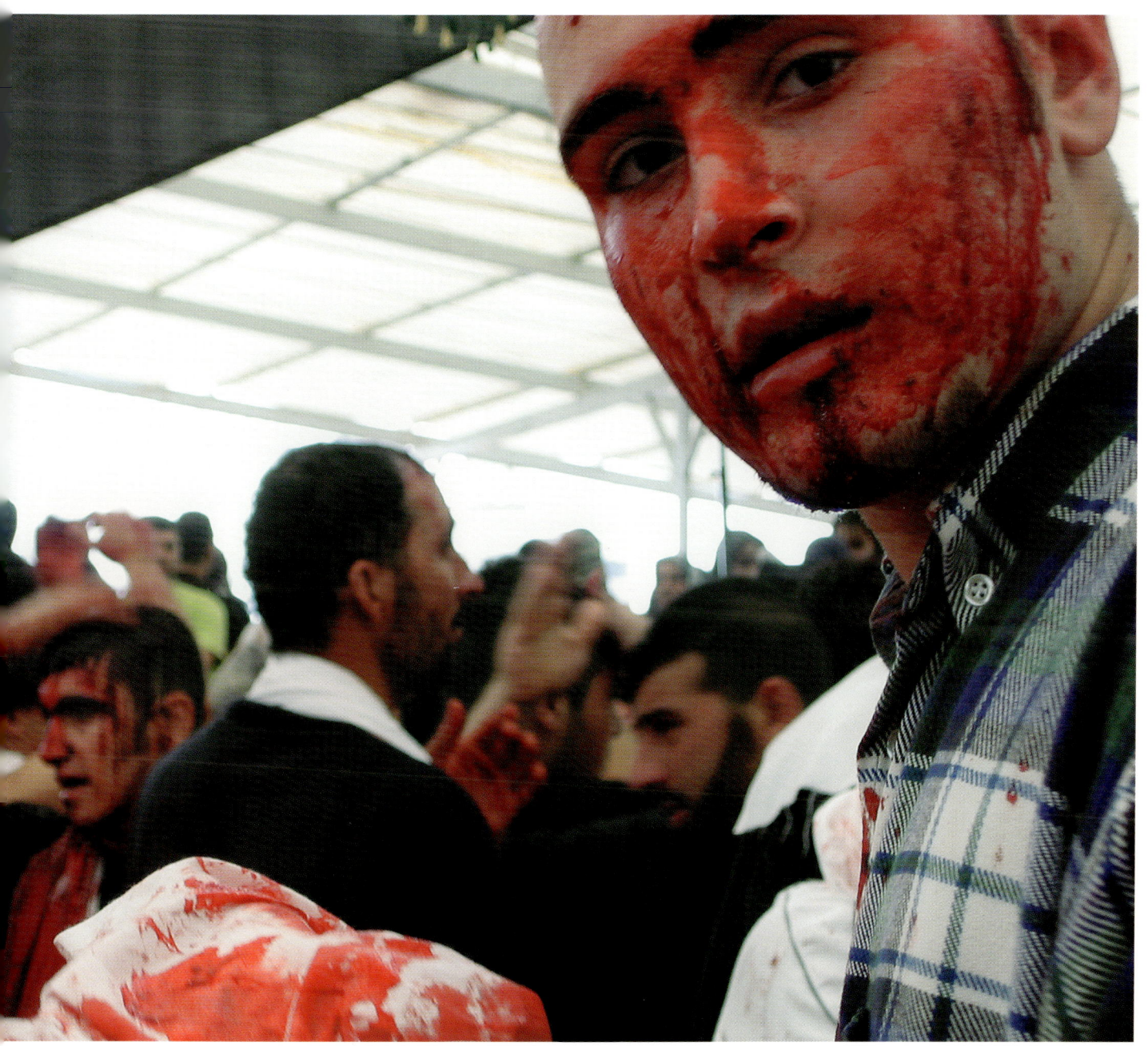

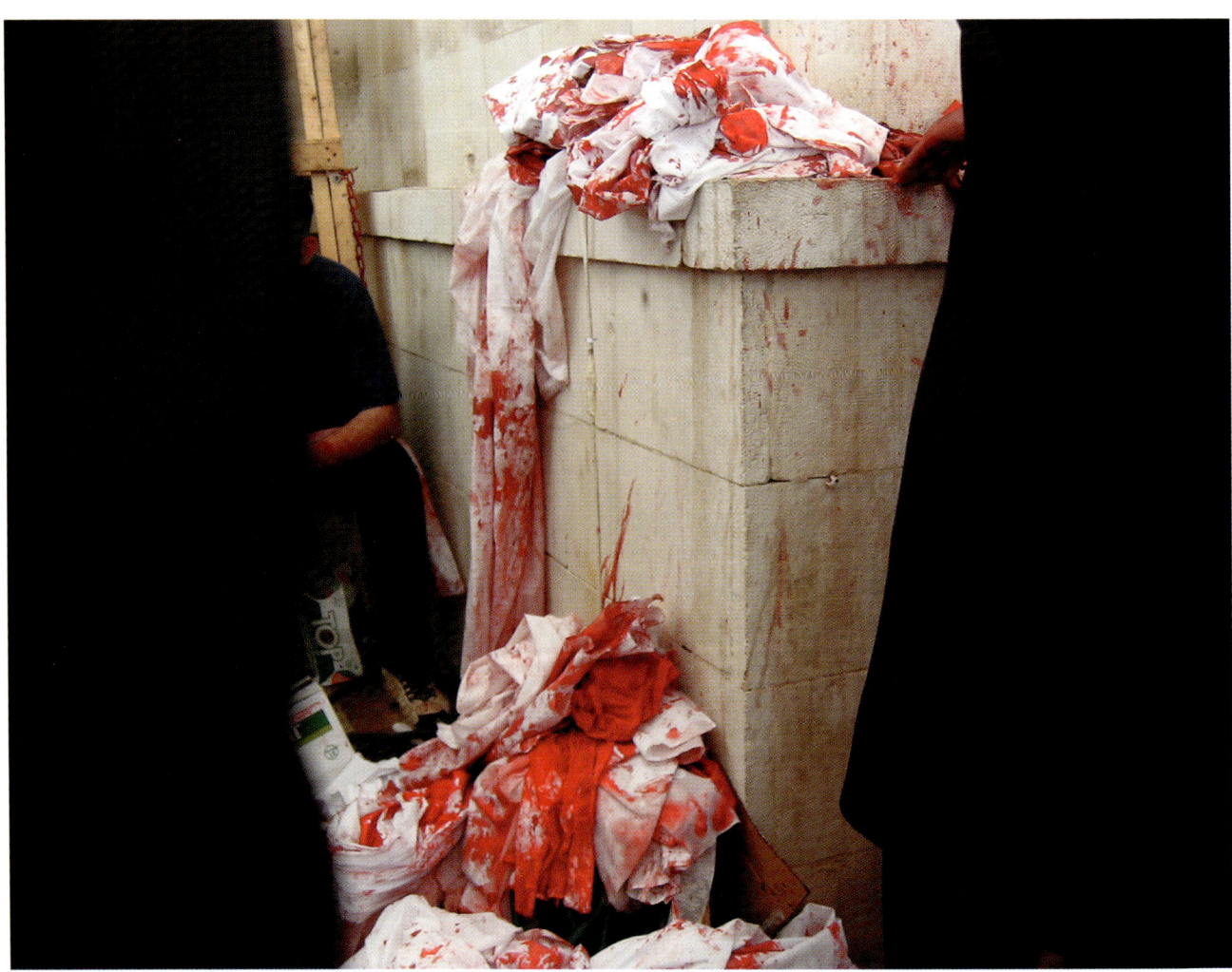

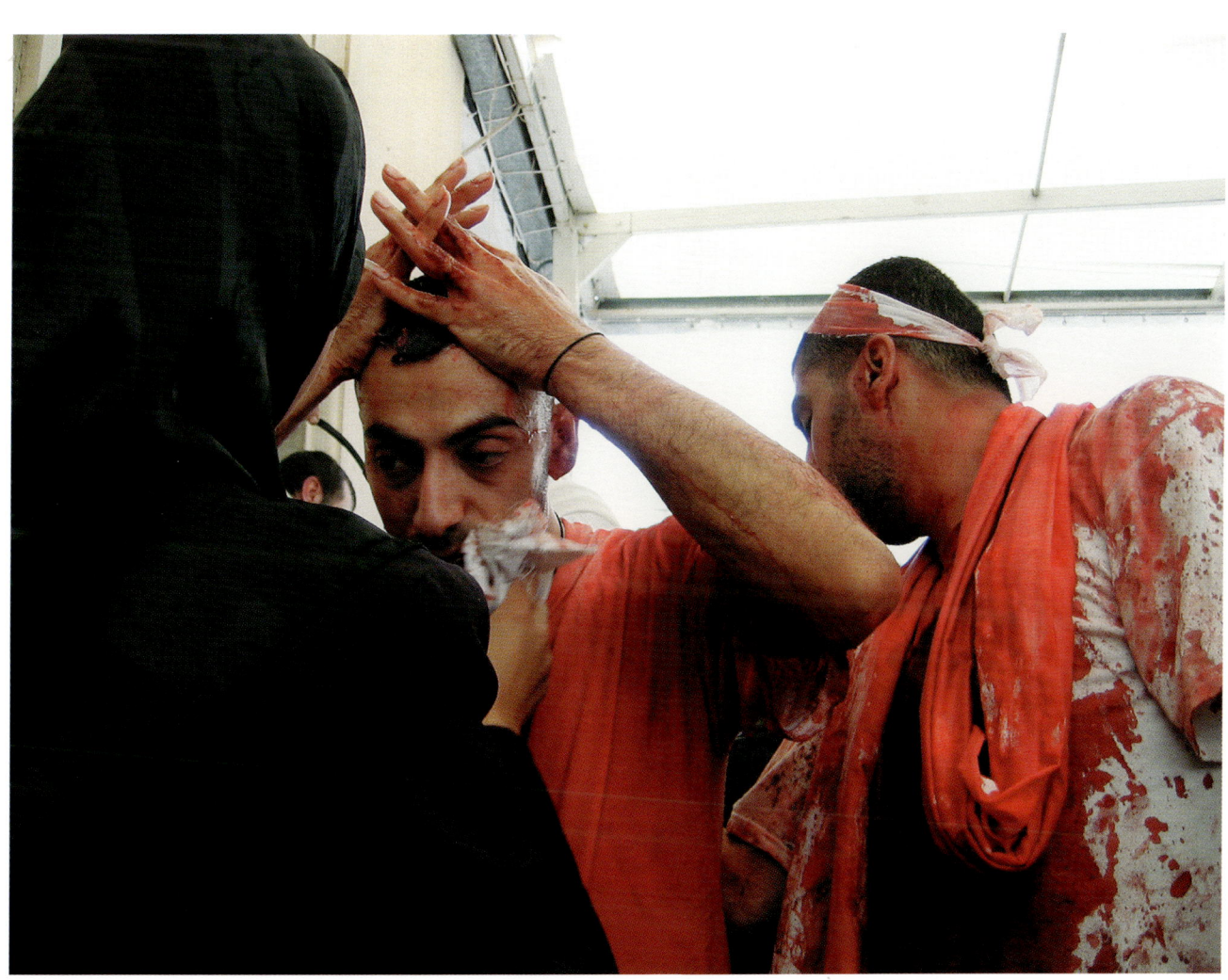

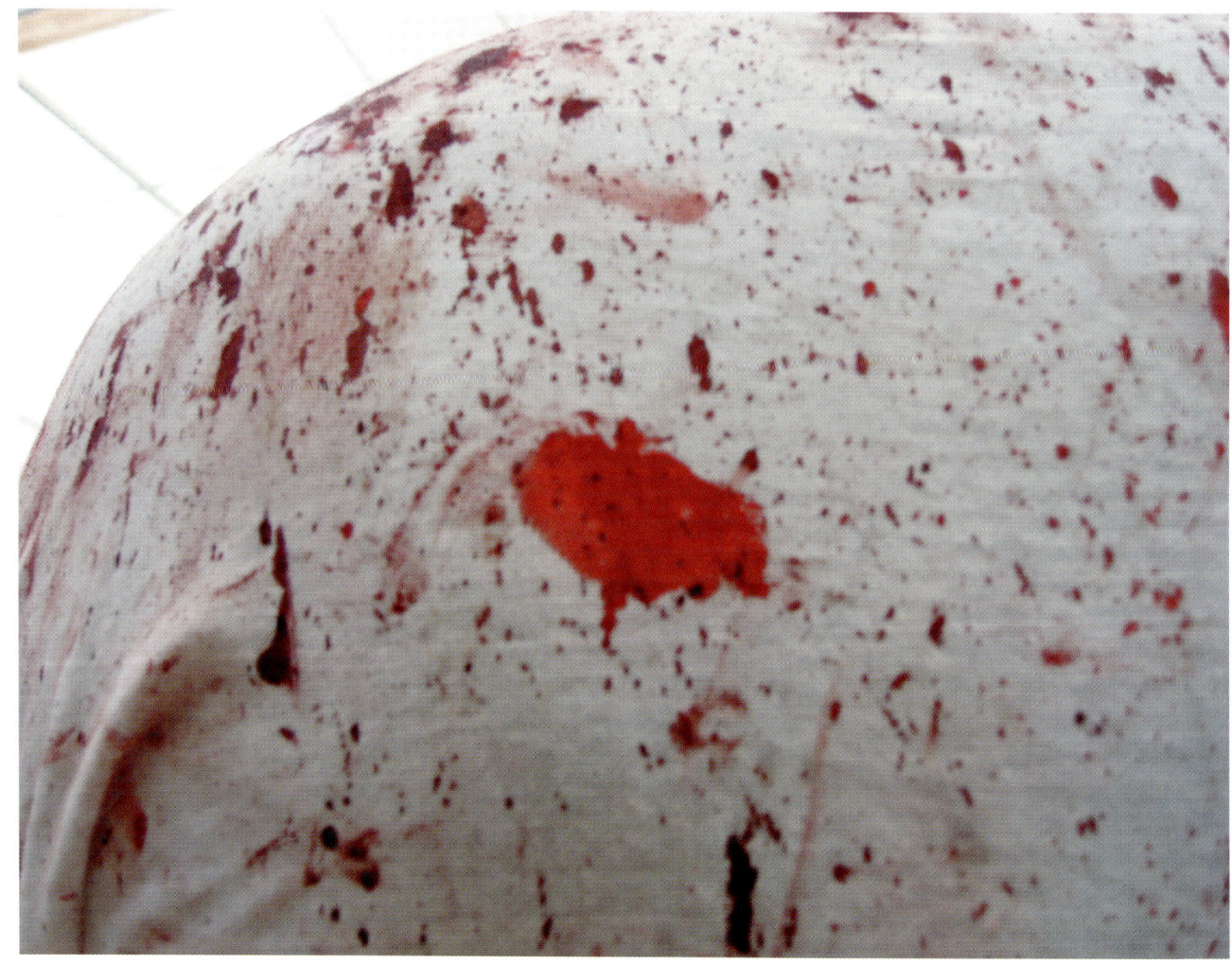

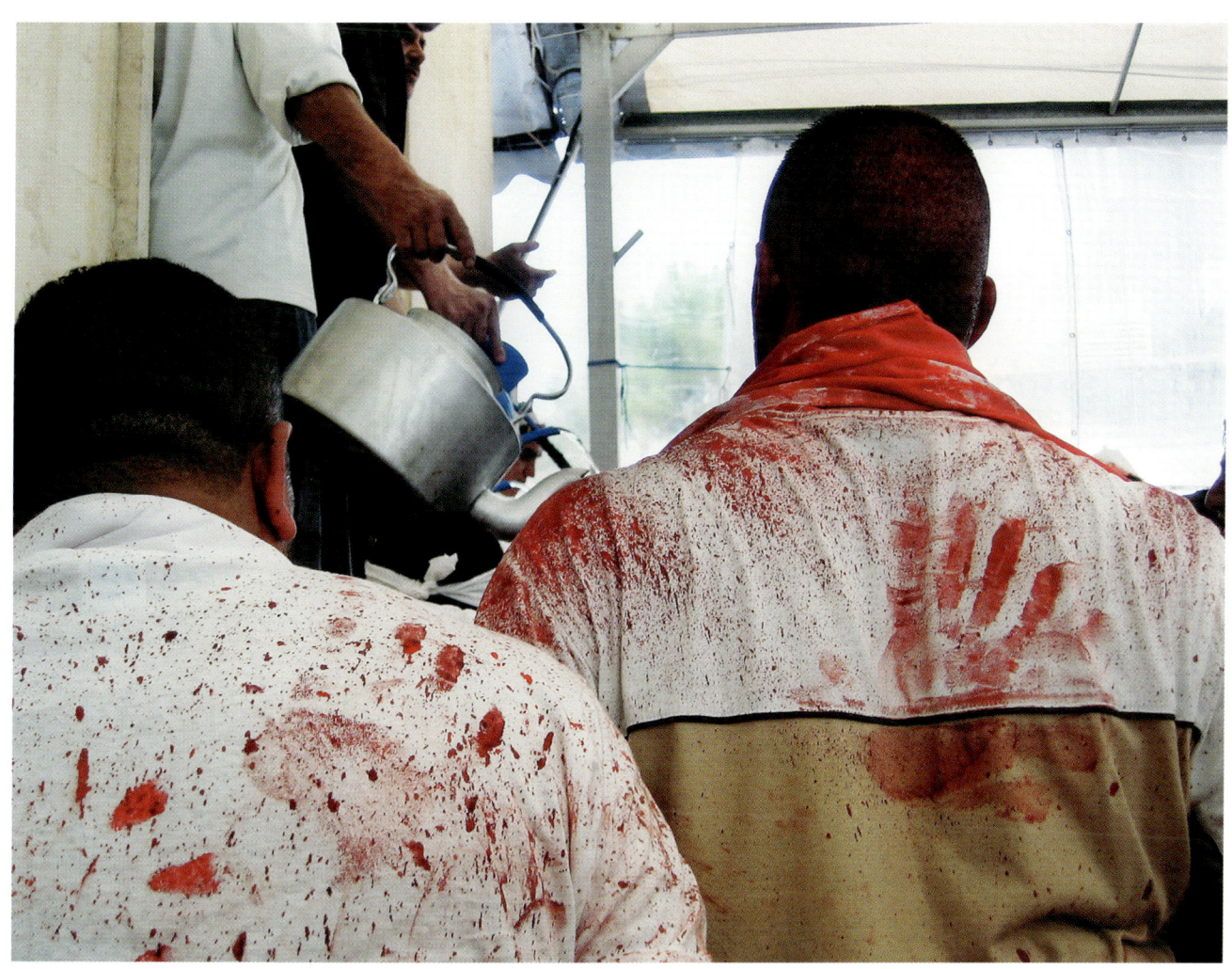

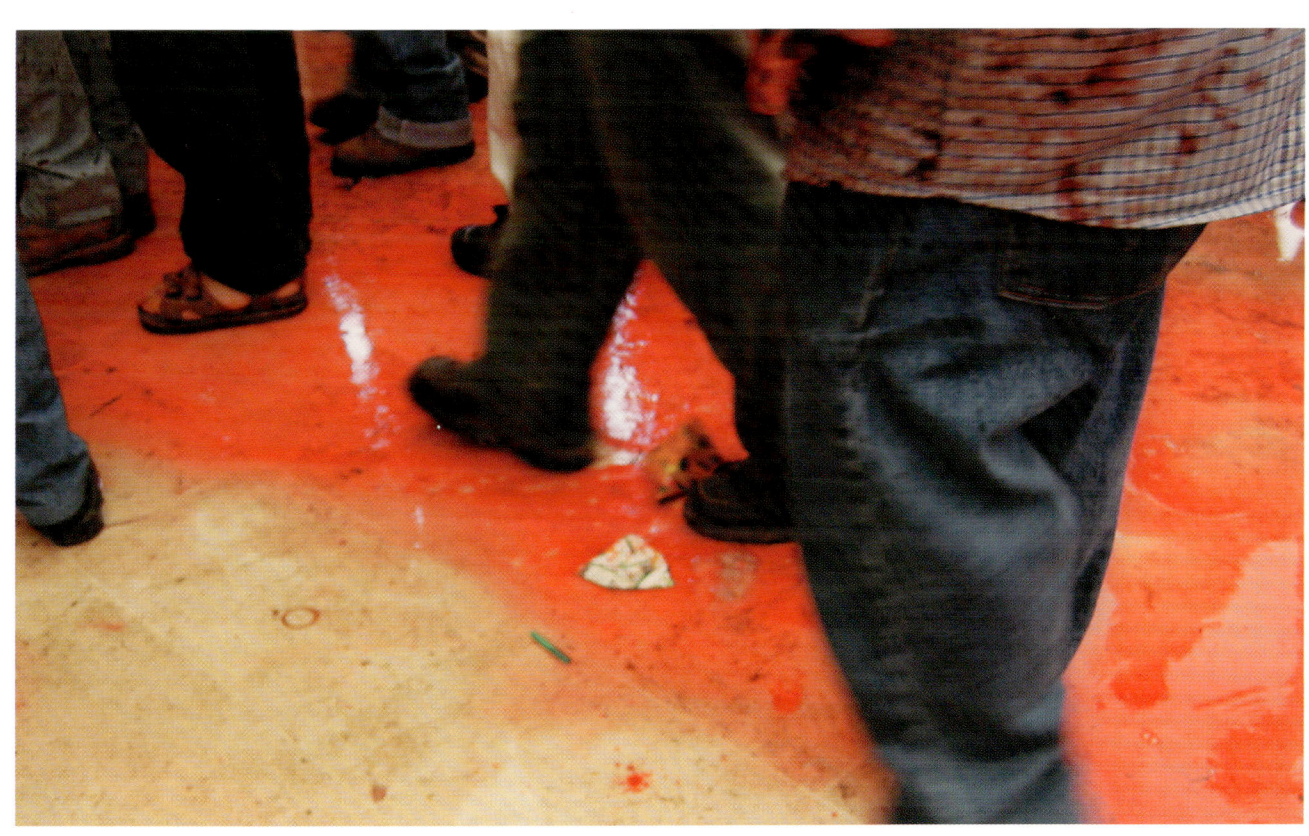

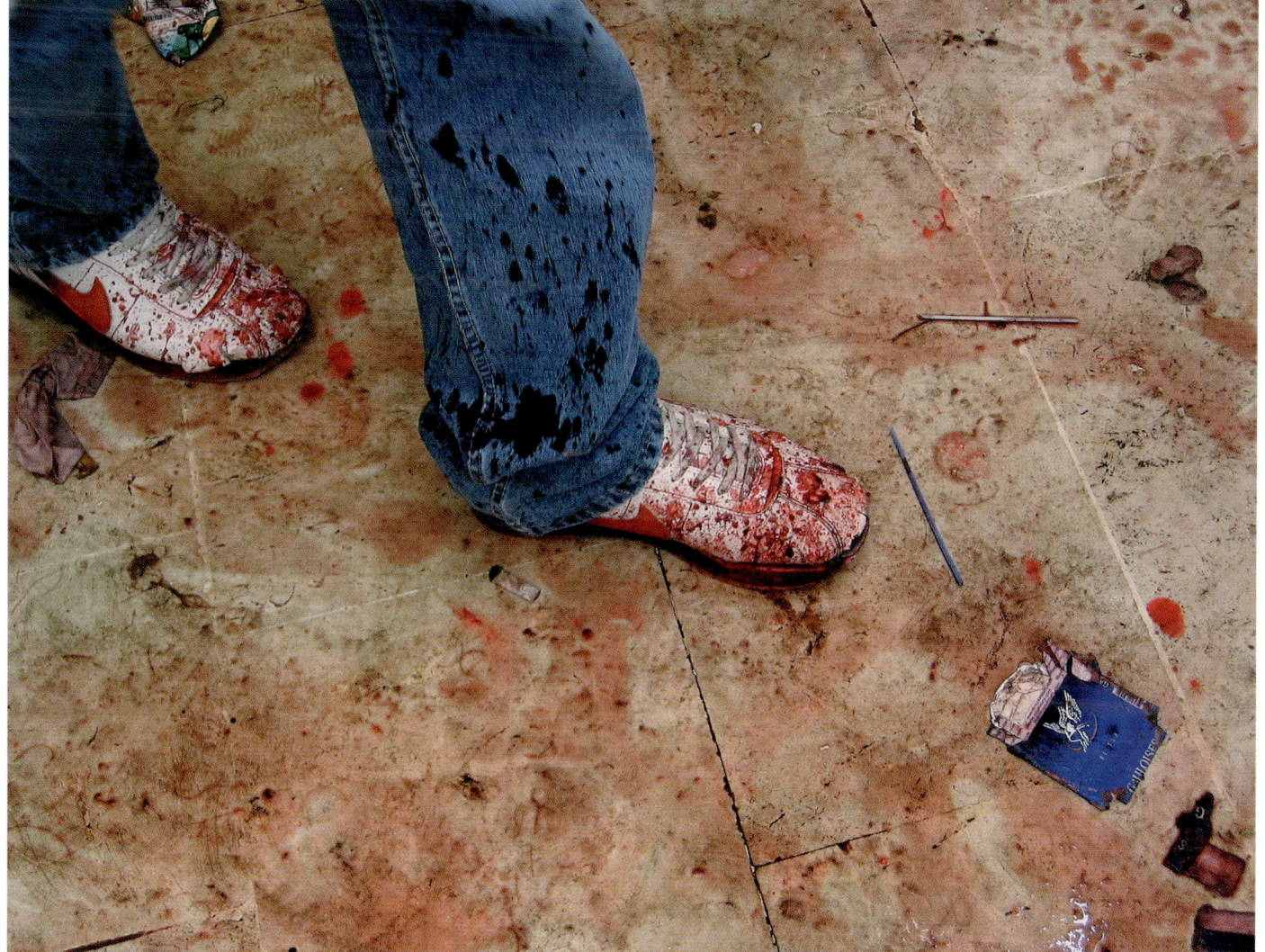

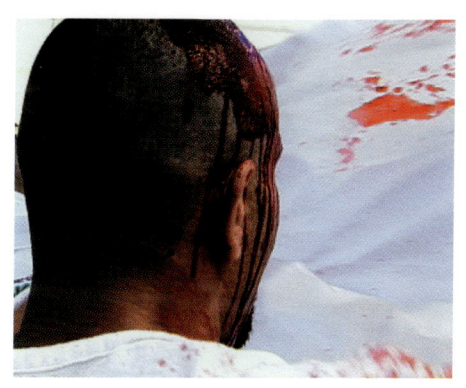

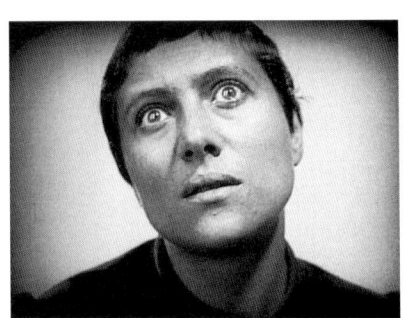

You have said that St. Michael appeared to you. In what form?

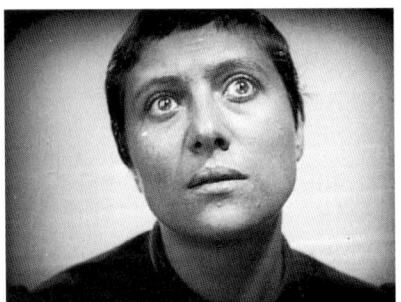

Did he have wings?

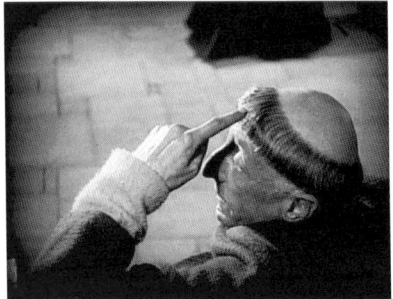
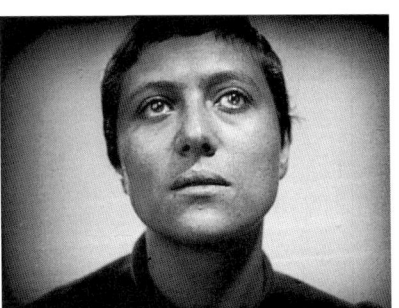

Did he wear a crown?

Stills from Dreyer's *The Passion of Joan of Arc*

Martyrs

Dedicated to mountain Tûr (aka Mount Sinai), one of the first martyrs[24]

We urgently need many more *shuhadâ'* in the contemporary Muslim world!

In order not to cheapen acts and states, we have to make sure that we don't cheapen the words we use to describe them.[25] In both the English *martyr* and the Arabic *shahîd* there is a conjunction of witnessing and death. "*Shâhid* and *Shahîd*: *One who tells*, or *gives information of*, *what he has witnessed*, or *seen or beheld with his eye*: *one who declares what he knows*: *a witness*, as meaning *one who gives testimony*, or *evidence*… [*one who gives decisive information*]. *Shahîd*: *A martyr who is slain in the cause of God's religion*… *al-Shahîd* as a name of God means *The Faithful*, or *Trusty*, *in his testimony*. *Shahâda*: *Information of what one has witnessed*, or *seen or beheld with his eye*: this is the primary signification… *Martyrdom in the cause of God's religion*."[26] And *martyr*, which comes from late Greek *martur*, meaning "witness," also means "one who chooses to suffer death rather than renounce religious principles."[27] Is this conjunction of witnessing and death accidental? No; does not the Qur'ân state: "And the agony of death cometh in truth.… (And unto the evil-doer it is said): Thou wast in heedlessness of this. Now We have removed from thee thy covering, and piercing is thy sight this day" (Qur'ân 50:19-22)? Notwithstanding the banners one sees in Lebanon during the Twelver Shi'ite yearly ten-day commemoration 'Âshûrâ, not *everyday is 'Âshûrâ*, and not *every land is Karbalâ*, but we will all be martyrs sooner or later. "Some men are born posthumously," writes Nietzsche in *The Antichrist*; I would add, most men and women die posthumously, i.e. are posthumous martyrs.[28] Do evil-doers die in order to have piercing sight, they whom "God has set a seal upon their hearts and ears; their sight is dimmed and grievous punishment awaits them" (Qur'ân

2:6-8)? Is it then out of His mercy, which "embraces everything" (Qur'ân 7:156), that God makes them die? Do the dead feel guilty and encounter "wrathful deities" because they were evil-doers while physically alive? Isn't it rather the case that in the death realm one feels insidious and unexplainable guilt and encounters wrathful deities whatever one did while physically alive? In which case it is only the one who dies before dying physically, achieving thus piercing sight and consequently not having to undergo the death realm, who is de jure not an evil-doer beyond his physical death. The prophet Muhammad, who would say on waking up, "Praise be to God, who hath revived us after putting us to death, and to Whom is the Resurrection,"[29] died before dying physically every night, more specifically at the onset of his night journey (*isrâ'*) from the sanctuary in Mecca to Jerusalem and thenceforth, beyond (sublunar) night and day, to Heaven (*mi'râj*): "Mâlik b. Sa'sa'a… said that God's Prophet, may God bless him, spoke to them about his Night Journey, 'While I was lying at the Hatîm [the curved wall that encompasses the Ka'ba on the north-west side]… suddenly someone came to me and slit me… from here to here.' — I said to al-Jârûd, who was by my side, 'What does he mean by that?' He said, 'He means from where the windpipe commences in the uppermost part of the breast to the place of growth of the hair beneath the navel,' or said, 'From the breastbone to the pubes.' — 'He then took out my heart. Then a gold tray filled with belief was brought to me and my heart was washed and was filled [with belief]. Then a white animal that's smaller than a mule and bigger than a donkey… and that places its foot at the farthest extent of its vision with each new step was brought to me, and I was carried over it. Gabriel set out with me until we reached the nearest heaven"[30] then the six other heavens, then the threshold beyond which Gabriel could not proceed. Then the prophet Muhammad "drew close, so He [God] came down, and he was two bows' length away, or closer" (Qur'ân 53:8-9). If the purpose of death is to give one piercing sight,[31] then, being already a *shahîd* in the fullest sense during his physical life, having experienced a Heavenly Ascension, the prophet Muhammad did not need to be part of the death realm past his physical demise. "When the news [of the Prophet's death] reached Abû Bakr [the future first Caliph]… he went [straight] to the Messenger of God in 'Â'ishah's house where he was lying in a corner… then said, '… Indeed, you have tasted the death which God had decreed for you. No [other] death will ever overtake you.'"[32] These words apply also to the first Shi'ite imâm, 'Alî b. Abî Tâlib, who is reported to have said, "Were the covering unveiled, I would not increase in certainty," and who while praying was fatally wounded by the Khârijî 'Abd al-Rahmân ibn Muljam on 27 January 661, dying two days later (Ibn Muljam, who was soon after executed by 'Alî's followers, is no martyr). If imâm Husayn, the grandson of a *shahîd*, the messenger of God Muhammad, and the son of a *shahîd*, imâm 'Alî, is also a martyr, indeed the Master of Martyrs according to Twelver Shi'ites, this should not be only in the sense that his dying in the way of God in Karbalâ' on 10 Muharram AH 61 (10 October 680) was exemplary, but also and basically because he saw with a piercing sight, and not only his coming death: "I know the day and hour, and the spot wherein I shall be killed. I know the place whereon I shall fall, and the spot in which I shall be buried, as I know you [Umm Salama]." Those who proclaim him the Master of Martyrs should try to show others, possibly at the risk of their lives,[33] the theophanic, visionary dimension of imâm Husayn. The Sûfî Husayn ibn Mansûr al-Hallâj (d. 922) *is a shahîd,* for he saw with a piercing sight and was executed for declaring what he witnessed, for instance: "I am the True Reality (God)" (*Anâ al-Haqq*). "They led him from the prison… (to the esplanade) where they cut off his hands and feet, after having flogged him with 500 lashes of the whip. Then he was hoisted up onto the cross (*suliba*)…. Abû Bakr Shiblî… said to him: 'What is Sûfîsm?' He answered: 'The lowest degree one needs for attaining it is the one that you behold.' Shiblî asked further: 'What is the highest degree?' Hallâj responded: 'It is out of reach for you; but tomorrow you will see; for it is part of the (divine) mercy that I have seen it and that it remains hidden to you.' At the time of the evening prayer (*'ishâ'*), the authorization by the Caliph to decapitate Hallâj came. But it was declared: 'It is too late; we shall put it off until tomorrow.' When morning came, they took him down from the gibbet…. His head was cut off, then his trunk was rolled up in a straw mat, doused with fuel, and burned. Later, they carried his ashes to Ra's al-Manâra, to disperse them to the wind."[34] The Nizârî Hasan *'ala dhikrihi'l-salâm* (on his mention be peace), who proclaimed the Great Resurrection in Alamût on 8 August 1164, ushering the unveiling of all that was occulted, and making exoteric all that was previously, in the cycles of occultation, esoteric, and who was shortly after viewed as the awaited *Qâ'im* (Resurrector), thus the epiphany of the *Haqîqa* (Truth/God), and who was assassinated in 1166 by a brother in-law, is one of Islam's greatest martyrs (his assassin, Hasan b. Nâmâwar, who was put to death by Hasan *'ala dhikrihi'l-salâm*'s great successor, his son the imâm Nûr al-Dîn Muhammad II, is not a martyr). Marco Polo writes of another leader of the Nizârîs: "In a beautiful valley enclosed between two lofty mountains, he had formed a luxurious garden…. at certain times he caused opium to be administered to ten or a dozen of the youths; and when half dead with sleep he had them conveyed to the several apartments of the palaces in the garden. Upon awakening from the state of lethargy… each perceived himself surrounded by lovely damsels, singing, playing, and attracting his regards by the most fascinating caresses, serving him also with delicate viands and exquisite wines; until intoxicated with excess of enjoyment amidst actual rivulets of milk and wine, he believed himself assuredly in Paradise… When four or five days had thus been passed, they were thrown once more into a state of somnolency, and carried out of the garden. Upon their being introduced to his presence, and questioned by him as to where they had been, their answer was, 'In Paradise…' (…) The chief thereupon addressing them, said: 'We have the assurances of our prophet that he who defends his lord shall inherit Paradise, and if you show yourselves devoted to the obedience of my orders, that happy lot awaits you.' The consequence of this system was, that when any of the neighbouring princes, or others, gave umbrage to this chief, they were put to death by these his disciplined assassins…"[35] Notwithstanding the inclusion in this bigoted account of many of the falsifications and misunderstandings found in numerous Christian medieval legends concerning the Nizârî Ismâ'îlîs,[36] it is valuable because it symptomatically implies correctly that the (Nizârî) *shahîd* is a visionary. In principle, it is not only the Nizârîs who died physically in assassination attempts against their enemies during the period of the Great Resurrection who are martyrs; any Nizârî who died physically in Alamût or any of the other Nizârî strongholds that proclaimed the Great Resurrection is a *shahîd*. When I used the expression "martyring operations" in my essay "I Am the Martyr Sanâ' Yûsif Muhaydlî" on the uncanny prerecorded introductory statement with which many of the Lebanese resistance fighters used to announce their bombing operations in south Lebanon against the Israeli army and/or the now-defunct South Lebanon Army (SLA), I was merely translating literally the Arabic expression "*'amaliyyât istishhâdiyya*," rather than indicating my own view of such operations; since to die before witnessing with a piercing sight is to commit suicide, I consider that the majority if not all of the aforementioned operations are actually suicidal operations (from another perspective, they can [also] be considered ransoming operations [*'amaliyyât fidâ'iyya*]). Following the death of four Israelis in the suicide bombing carried out by Rîm al-Riâshî, the mother of a three-year-old son and a one-year-old daughter, at the Erez border crossing between the Gaza Strip and Israel, Ze'ev Boim, Israel's deputy defence minister, told Israeli army radio on 16 January 2004: "Sheikh [Ahmad] Yassin [founder and ideological leader of the Palestinian Islamic movement Hamâs] is marked for death, and he should hide himself deep underground where he won't know the difference between day and night" (*The Independent*, 17 January 2004). In response, shaykh Ahmad Yâsîn declared: "Death threats do not frighten us, we are in search of martyrdom." (Ibid.) The quadriplegic man was assassinated on 22 March by missiles, fired from Israeli helicopter gunships, on leaving from dawn prayers in Gaza City. His obituary in *Al-Ahram Weekly*'s 25 - 31 March 2004 issue was titled: "The Martyr Sheikh." Palestinian President Yâsir 'Arafât's response to threats by

Israeli Prime Minister Ariel Sharon was: 'All of us are martyrs-in-the-waiting'" (*Guardian*, 25 April 2004). At a rally "in defense of the religious holy Shi'ite sites in Karbalâ' and Najaf against the US-led occupying forces in Iraq" that was attended by over a hundred thousand people covered in white shrouds in Beirut's predominantly Shi'ite southern suburb on 21 May 2004, Hasan Nasr Allâh, the secretary general of the Party of God (*Hizb Allâh*), said: "This time we march symbolically in shrouds, the next time, when our oppressed brethren call upon us for help, we shall dress in shrouds and arms" (*The Daily Star*, 22 May 2004). On Friday 7 May 2004, the 31-year-old Shi'ite cleric Muqtadâ al-Sadr, the most ignorant, inarticulate and inelegant of post-Saddâm Husayn Iraq's Shi'ite leaders, who led a counterproductive insurgency against the occupying Coalition Forces in Iraq in 2004,[37] gave his sermon at the main mosque in Kûfa with his shoulders draped with a white coffin shroud symbolizing his readiness for martyrdom, and said a short while later: "I wish to be a martyr, and I don't fear death."[38] Can one legitimately say: unable to give anything else, I can still (at most) give my life? No, since one cannot give life unless He is the one who created it in the first place (Allâh/God the Father) or he is life (Jesus Christ, the Son of God: "I am the resurrection and the life" [John 11:25]). In a lesser sense, since at a lower level, only the one who has achieved piercing sight by dying before dying physically can give his life in a battle (consequently neither Rîm al-Riâshî nor shaykh Ahmad Yâsîn gave their lives for Palestine),[39] since to him, a *shahîd* prior to his physical demise, apply the words of Qur'ân 3:169: "Call not those who are slain in the way of Allah 'dead.' Nay, they are living…" As long as one has not achieved piercing sight, i.e. as long as one belongs to those who "though seeing, they do not see; though hearing, they do not hear or understand" (Matthew 13:13),[40] i.e. as long as one is not truly alive, and therefore cannot give one's "life,"[41] one has to flee "life"-threatening situations, more precisely embark on a (Deleuze and Guattari) *line of flight*,[42] as some of prophet Muhammad's persecuted followers did by emigrating from Mecca to Abyssinia. Did Moses lead the Hebrews into an armed rebellion against the Pharaoh? This would have been premature, suicidal. He rather led them into one of the great lines of flight, out of Egypt across Sinai. Some of the Jews who embarked on this line of flight became martyrs: "And when ye said: O Moses! We will not believe in thee till we see Allah plainly; and even while ye gazed the lightning seized you. Then We revived you after your extinction, that ye might give thanks" (Qur'ân 2:55-56). With the exception of Moses and Aaron, were the contemporaries of these Jews aware that the latter were alive ("Call not those who are slain in the way of Allah 'dead.' Nay, they are living, only ye perceive not" [Qur'ân 3:169])? I very much doubt it. The 1980s Belfast graffito **IS THERE LIFE BEFORE DEATH?** is one of the major questions that the "contemporary" Middle East, a region both seemingly largely convinced that there is life after death and wallowing in nihilism, should confront. Could Rîm al-Riâshî, shaykh Ahmad Yâsîn, or former Lebanese prime minister Rafîq al-Harîrî have answered this question with a definitive "Yes!"? No, only *shuhadâ'*/martyrs can do so (being—like the vast majority of humans, who deferred dying until their physical demise and thus are appropriately called *the late*—merely posthumous martyrs, Rîm al-Riâshî, shaykh Ahmad Yâsîn, and assassinated former Lebanese prime minister Rafîq al-Harîrî can only answer the question "Is there life *after* death?"). It is symptomatic of how intensely alive is the real witness, the one who has piercing sight, that there are bound to be some discerning people who, at least transiently, do not believe in his or her physical death. When the Messenger of God died physically, 'Umar b. al-Khattâb, the future second caliph, stood up saying, "Some of the hypocrites allege that the Messenger of God is dead. By God, he is not dead, but has gone to his Lord as Moses b. 'Imrân went and remained hidden from his people for forty days. Moses returned after it was said that he had died. By God, the Messenger of God will [also] return…"[43] Notwithstanding the assassination of 'Alî b. Abî Tâlib, Abdu'llâh ibn Sabâ al-Himyarî and his followers, the Sabâi'iyya, denied that 'Alî had died, affirming that he would return to fill the Earth with justice.[44] Jesus Christ, the son of Mary but not of God, this great visionary who opened the eyes of a number of blind people ("I heal him who was born blind… by Allah's leave" [Qur'ân 3:49]),[45] and who is one of the greatest martyrs of Islam ("Allah took him up unto Himself… and on the Day of Resurrection he will be a witness against them [because of their saying: We slew the Messiah, Jesus son of Mary, Allah's messenger]" [Qur'ân 4:157-159]), did not die on the cross according to Moslems ("They slew him [the Messiah, Jesus son of Mary, Allah's messenger] not nor crucified him, but it appeared so unto them…" [Qur'ân 4:157]).[46] Many of Hallâj's supporters and disciples denied that he had died, and "began to make preparations for his return after forty days…. And one of Hallâj's disciples maintained that the one who had been executed was an enemy of Hallâj, changed to look like him (Ibn Sinân: just as in the case of Jesus, son of Mary). Some of them claimed that they had seen him the very next day… mounted on a donkey…"[47] So, a year after Hallâj's execution, his head was dispatched by the authorities in Baghdad to Khurasan and carried around from district to district to convince his supporters there of his execution.[48]

Given the many unjust and humiliating conditions that are the daily experience of Palestinians in the Occupied Territories, what is the moment that suddenly felt unbearable for one or more Palestinians, that stopped the interior monologue, that broke the sensory-motor link?[49] From June 2002, he, a Palestinian living in the West Bank, followed with apprehension the news about the construction by the Israeli government of Ariel Sharon of a "Security Fence" ostensibly to block terrorist attacks. He saw the "Security Fence" progress day after day, discovering that it was actually an 8-meter-tall wall with razor-fringed fencing, watchtowers every few hundred meters, and buffer zones on either side, and that it encroached on substantial areas of the West Bank. Remembering Nietzsche's characterization of Jesus of Nazareth as "the peaceful preacher of the mount, the seashore and the fields, who appears like a new Buddha on a soil very unlike India's…" (*The Antichrist*), he wondered whether one could be a Taoist on a soil very unlike China's, namely the West Bank;[50] and whether, as in Taoism, where "the movements of the painter's brush must be interrupted [without interruption of the breath that is animating them]" (Li Jih-Hua),[51] a Palestinian could maintain the *chi* (vital breath/original energy) without a break despite some 700 checkpoints operational in the West Bank and Gaza in December 2003, which often closed for good for weeks, and which even when open often took hours to cross—and now despite the Wall of Separation. For a period of several weeks, he was obsessed by Borges' "The Wall and the Books": "I read, a few days ago, that the man who ordered the building of the almost infinite Chinese Wall was that first Emperor, Shih Huang Ti, who also decreed the burning of all the books that had been written before his time.[52] That these two vast undertakings—the five or six hundred leagues of stone against the barbarians, and the rigorous abolition of history, that is, of the past—were the work of the same person and were, in a sense, his attributes, inexplicably satisfied and, at the same time, disturbed me.… Herbert Allen Giles recounts that anyone who concealed books was… condemned to work on the endless wall until the day of his death."[53] He thought that one could paraphrase Borges' words thus within the context of Israeli politics: the man who ordered the building of the Wall of Separation was that Israeli prime minister, Ariel Sharon, who also decreed the burning of all the books relating to the Palestinians: during the Israeli invasion of Lebanon in 1982, when Sharon was Israel's defense minister, the Israeli army seized and possibly destroyed the archives of the Palestine Research Center in Beirut, and during the Israeli reoccupation of the Gaza strip beginning in late March 2002, Israeli military forces destroyed or seized the computers, books, audio recordings, videos, institutional archives and records housed in many Palestinian cultural resources. That these two vast undertakings—the 788 kilometers of stone against "the barbarians," and the rigorous abolition of history, that is, of the past of the Palestinian people—were the work of the same person and were, in a sense, his attributes inexplicably satisfied and, at the same time, disturbed him. He thought that sooner or later the destruction of books in an Israel that was turning increasingly right-wing, militaristic, and chauvinistic, and whose initial racism was becoming even more exacerbated, would apply not only to those that refer to and/or document the Palestinian past but also to those, archaeological or otherwise, that contradict the Bible, and then to all books other than the Bible, its orthodox interpretation("s") and the scientific and technological publications presenting the latest advances in certain cutting edge fields where Israeli scientists are making a significant contribution, for example nanotechnology.[54] At that point any Israeli who concealed books other than the aforementioned allowed ones would be condemned to work, until the day of his or her death, on the Wall of Separation, which would be constantly in need of repair since repeatedly sabotaged at various points by its victims, the Palestinians. Elsewhere in the same text, Borges writes: "Perhaps Shih Huang Ti condemned those who adored the past to a work as vast as the past, as stupid and as useless."[55] Similarly, perhaps Ariel Sharon is unwittingly condemning those in Israel who adore the past, namely the settlers in the Occupied Territories, who base their territorial claims on the Bible, to "a work as vast as the past, as stupid and as useless." He wondered whether, as with the Great Wall of China (aka 10,000 Li Long Wall), which was added to the UNESCO World Heritage List in 1987, the Security Wall (aka the Security Fence) will, if completed, be added one day to the same list. It may in the short term become a wailing wall for the Palestinians, but it is likely in the long term to become another Wailing Wall for the Israeli Jews, coming to rival and possibly to supplant the 50 meters long Wailing Wall in the Old City of Jerusalem (aka the Western Wall), the only remains of the Second Temple destroyed in 70, and which dates back to about the 2nd century BC (its upper sections were added later). On 23 February 2004, as the International Court of Justice in The Hague began hearings on the legality of Israel's Wall of Separation, he along with thousands of other Palestinians as well as international peace activists marched in protest against this Wall of Separation in various towns and villages in the West Bank and Gaza Strip.[56] In rare cases, one's disconnecting of the Wall of Separation from the mendacious justifications for its construction leads to the disconnection of the sensory functions from the motor ones in a breakdown of the sensory-motor link; more frequently, it is the breakdown of the sensory-motor link that leads to a concomitant disconnection of the Wall of Separation from not only the mendacious and mystifying justifications for its construction, but also from all the real reasons for its presence (encroaching on Palestinian territories; contributing toward rendering a viable Palestinian state on the Occupied Territories impossible; minimizing terrorist attacks against Israeli civilians; gaining political votes, since, according to many polls, over 70% of Israelis are in favor of the Wall of Separation, etc.). The Wall of Separation was so unbearable to him that it broke his sensory-motor link,[57] i.e. disconnected the sensory functions from the motor ones, and suspended his interior monologue, with voices and hallucinations coming to insert themselves in the gap between the sensory functions and the motor ones. Indeed, one not so fine day, while going to visit a friend, something anomalous obstructed his vision. It seemed to have suddenly appeared from one day to the next. He approached it with much trepidation. Was it a wall (for certainly it was not a fence)? Yes! It seemed never to end! Did it reach China and envelope its Great Wall? Did it circle the Earth? Was he losing his mind and hallucinating it? Or was he still sleeping and dreaming it? And if he was dreaming even when he thought he was awake, then how to wake up? He thought that this could be achieved only by death, for didn't the prophet Muhammad say: "People are asleep, and when they die, they awake"? A few days later, like others before him, he recorded a video testimony[58]—the task in the prerecorded video testimony of the one soon to embark on a bombing operation is to tell or intimate to his or her addressees what he or she has seen. Later that day, he blew himself up in a crowded bus, killing along with himself a number of Israelis (did the scene of the horrifying carnage in turn produce a breakdown of the sensory-motor link of some Israeli who happened to be passing there?).[59] It is both incumbent upon, and relevant for an Arab to condemn in no uncertain terms the indiscriminate killing by Palestinian suicide bombers of Israeli civilians living within Israel's 1967 borders (as well as both the indiscriminate slaughter of civilians and the targeted mass killings of Shi'ites in Iraq by suicide bombers from other Arab countries, many of whom are Wahhâbîs)[60] as long as these bombings are still *reactions*, whether political or revengeful or mimetic, or all of these conjointly. It is irrelevant to condemn such bombings—but not the unbearable conditions that give rise to them in the case of the Palestinians—when they are no longer reactions but an unpredictable by-product of the breakdown of the sensory-motor link, since while one can prevent a reaction, one cannot prevent an event.

André Bazin writes in "The Ontology of the Photographic Image": "If the plastic arts were put under psychoanalysis, the practice of embalming the dead might turn out to be a fundamental factor in their creation. The process might reveal that at the origin of painting and sculpture there lies a mummy complex…" Photographs are a way of preservation against death, but what would that way of preservation matter if in order to see them with a piercing sight, one that goes through so many veils, one would have to be already dead ("And the agony of death cometh in truth…. Thou wast in heedlessness of this. Now We have removed from thee thy covering, and piercing is thy sight this day" [Qur'ân 50:19-22])? Is the meeting of object and its (re)viewing with a piercing sight (is there a clear-cut difference between viewing and reviewing in death, where what one encounters has often the feel of something that is familiar while strange, or strange while familiar, *unheimilich*, uncanny?) necessarily missed? Not if we managed to die before dying, i.e. to become martyrs, *shuhadâ'*. Five paragraphs into Rilke's *The Notebook of Malte Laurids Brigge*, their twenty-eight-year-old eponymous diegetic author, who has just arrived in Paris, notes in his journal's fourth entry: "I am learning to see." On reading these words, I suspect that the notebook will trace the vicissitudes of his martyrdom. A few entries later, he again writes: "Have I said it before? I am learning to see." My suspicion is heightened by this reiteration, becoming virtually a certainty. And indeed, I suddenly recall the book's ominous beginning words: "People come here [Paris], then, to live? I should rather have thought that they came here to die."

Posthumous Martyrs

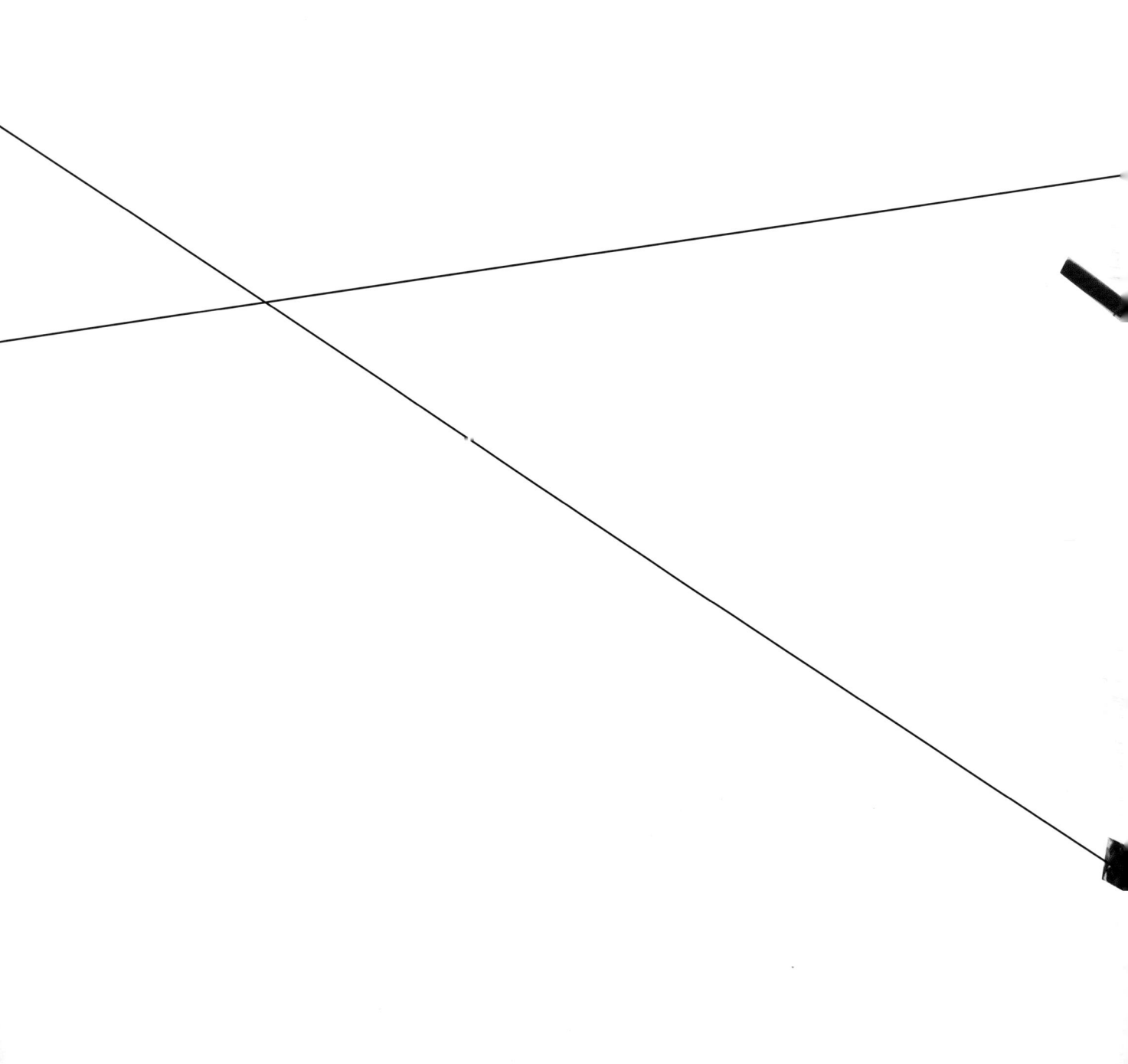

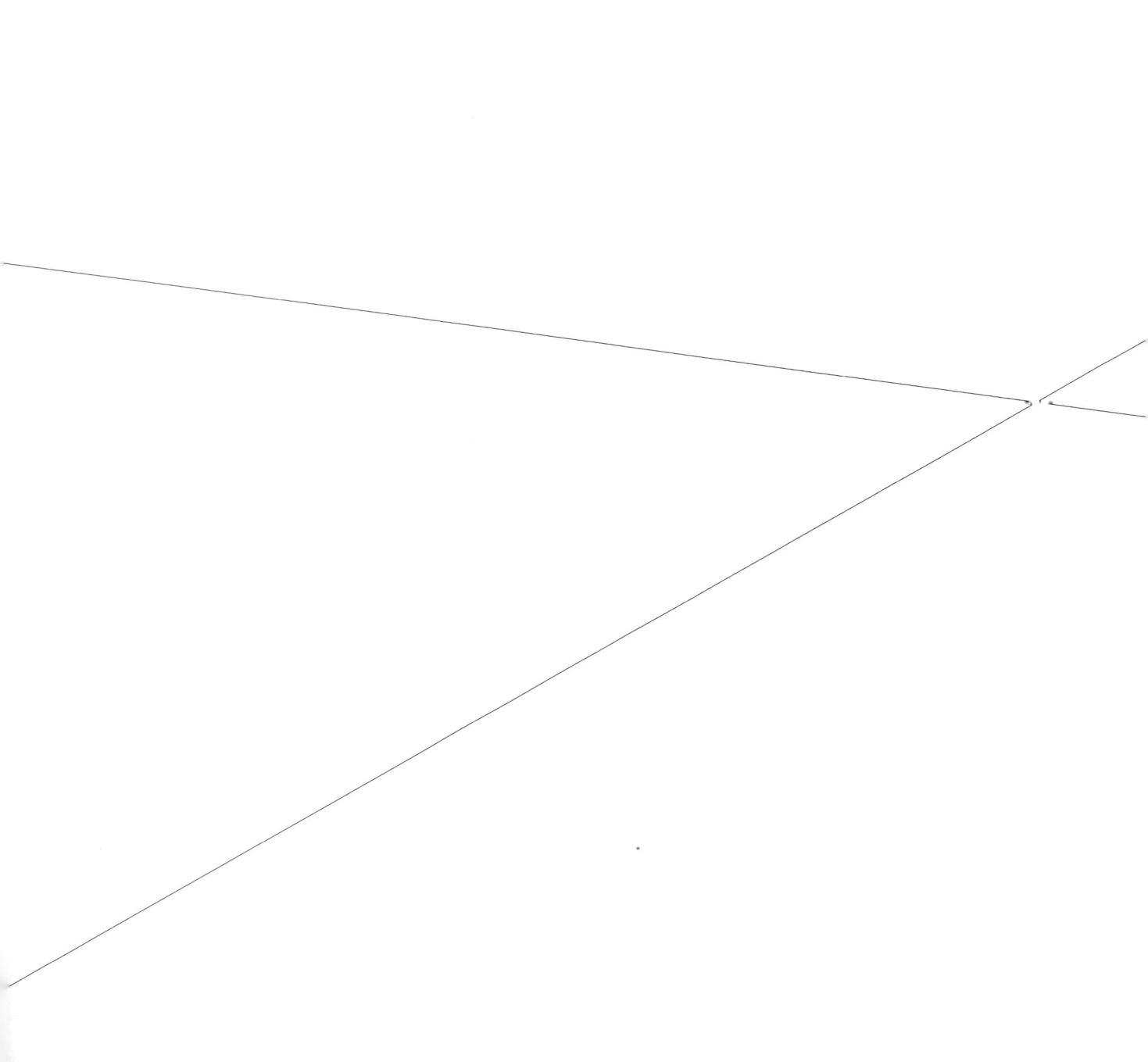

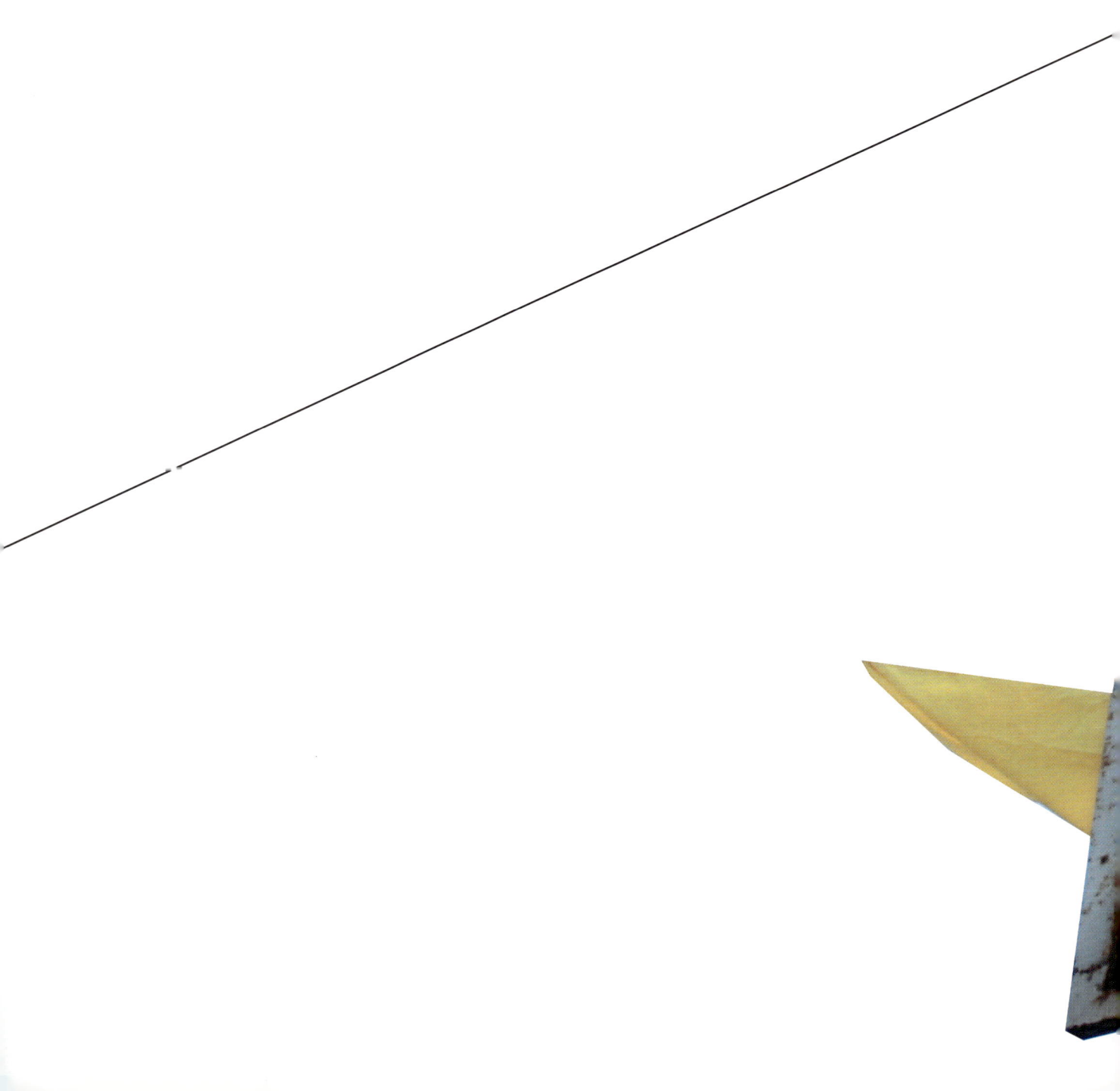

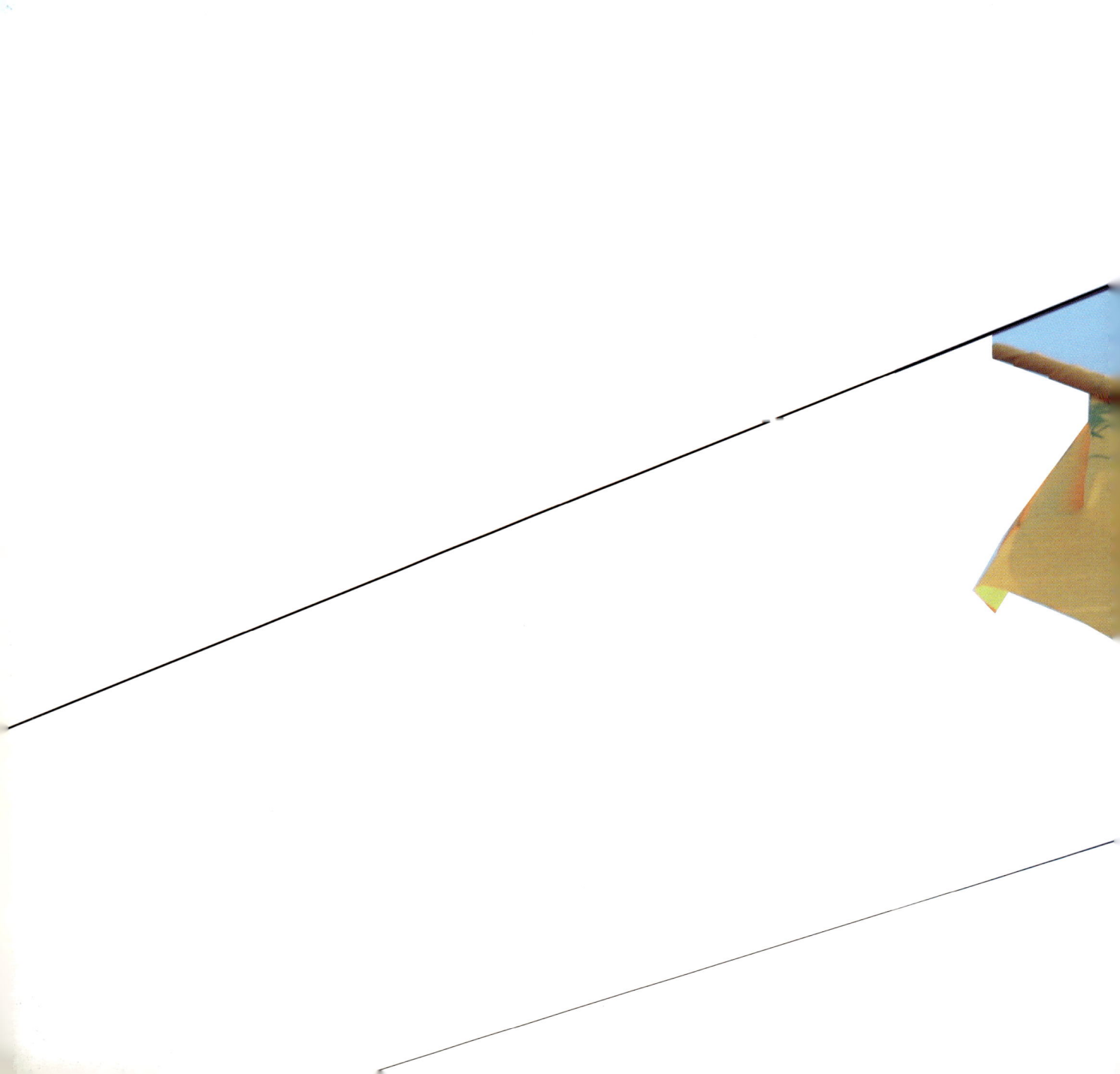

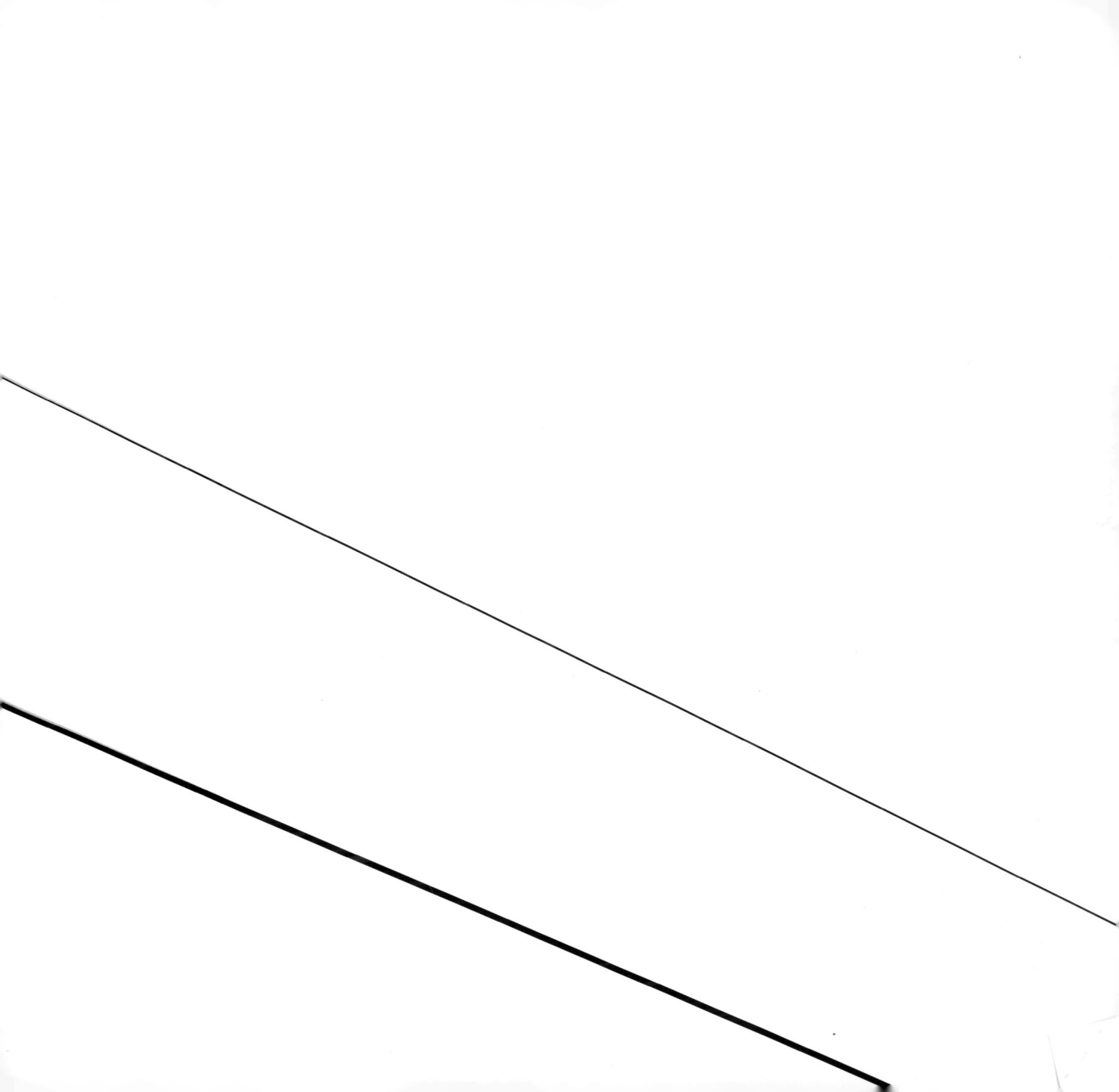

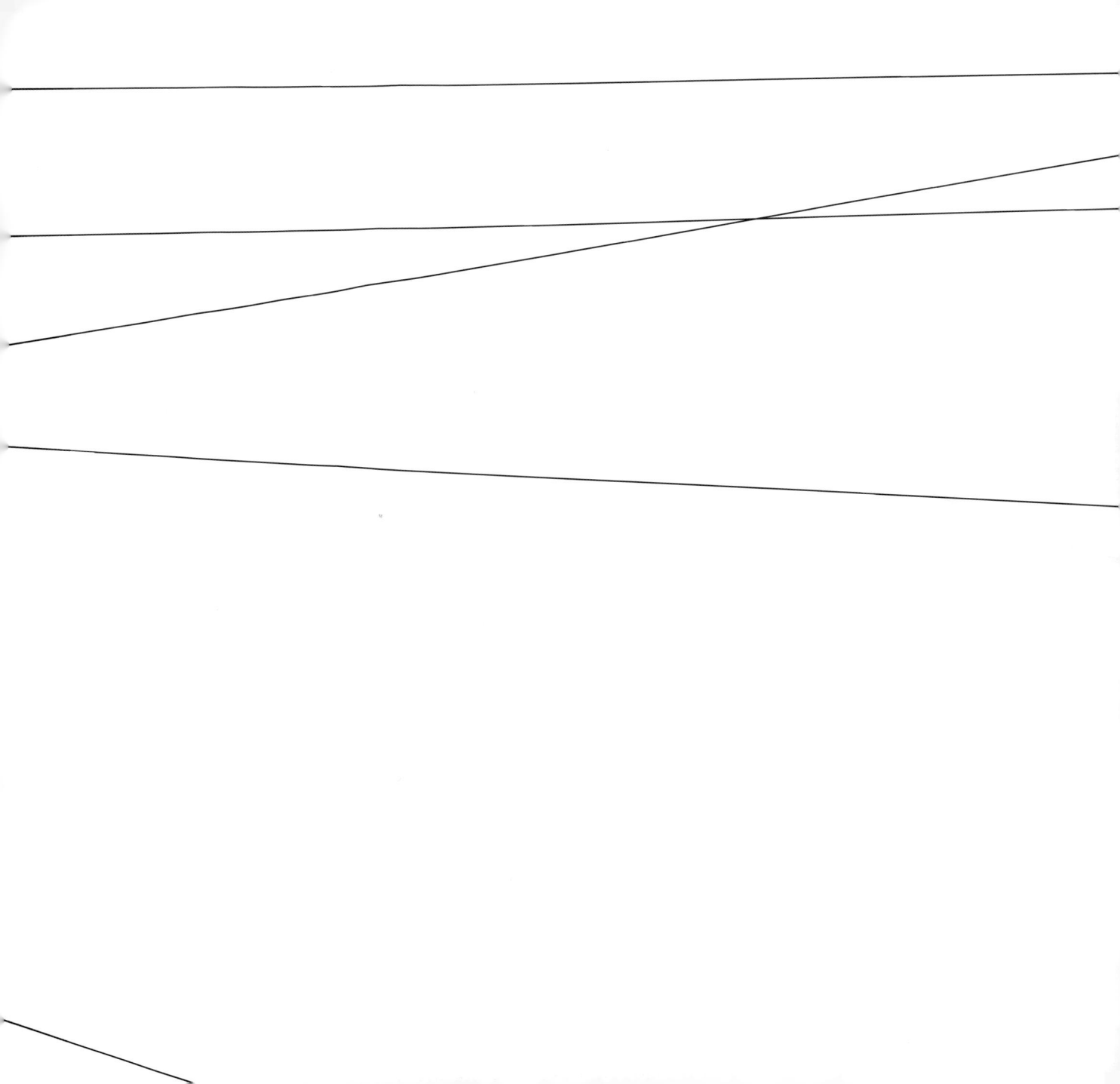

Notes

[1] Dōgen: "An ancient Buddha said: 'For the time being stand on top of the highest peak.... / For the time being three heads and eight arms. / For the time being an eight- or sixteen-foot body....' 'For the time being' here means time itself is being, and all being is time. A golden sixteen-foot body is time... 'Three heads and eight arms' is time... Yet an ordinary person who does not understand buddha-dharma may hear the words *the time-being* this way: 'For a while I was three heads and eight arms.... Even though the mountains and rivers still exist, I have already passed them... Those mountains and rivers are as distant from me as heaven is from earth.' It is not that simple. At the time the mountains were climbed and the rivers crossed, you were present. Time is not separate from you, and as you are present, time does not go away." ["The Time-Being" (*uji*)].

[2] Cf. "Freud does not consider this amnesia [infantile amnesia] to be the result of any functional inability of the young child to record his impressions; instead, he attributes it to the repression which falls upon infantile sexuality (...). Just like hysterical amnesia, infantile amnesia can in principle be dispelled; it does not imply any destruction or absence of registrations of memories..." (J. Laplanche and J.-B. Pontalis, *The language of Psycho-analysis*, trans. Donald Nicholson-Smith, with an introduction by Daniel Lagache [New York: Norton, 1973], pp. 212-213).

[3] Among other factors, we can call the long primeval period the "prehistory of man" for the following two complementary reasons. The first is that he had a flighty mind and was attuned only to the passing moment, and so was unable to produce the deep temporality of past/present/future required to construct a history. The second reason is that most of the torture to inculcate in him a memory, i.e. the most atrocious and frequent torture, was happening then, with the result that that period, the most traumatic of all, was and still is repressed, and consequently is not included in our history—it is as it were humanity's *infantile amnesia*.

[4] Nietzsche's words apply far better to the distant past, for man could then withstand much more pain because he was much

more superficial, whereas now, having to a large extent succeeded in creating a memory for himself and therefore being (temporally) far deeper, with few exceptions intense pain easily and quickly traumatizes him, ushering repression and consequently post-traumatic amnesia.

[5] A long-term memory of the addressee of the promise is a precondition even for the promiser. Thus one of the conditions for God's promise to Abraham is that the latter create a memory for himself: "Then God said, 'Take your son, your only son, Isaac, whom you love, and go to the region of Moriah. Sacrifice him there as a burnt offering on one of the mountains I will tell you about.' (…) The angel of the Lord called to Abraham from heaven a second time and said, 'I swear by myself, declares the Lord, that because you have done this and have not withheld your son, your only son, I will surely bless you and make your descendants as numerous as the stars in the sky and as the sand on the seashore. Your descendants will take possession of the cities of their enemies, and through your offspring all nations on earth will be blessed…' " (Genesis 22:2-18).

[6] Clearly castration is here theorized from a different perspective than the one encountered in most feminist film criticism drawing on psychoanalysis (see Laura Mulvey's "Visual Pleasure and Narrative Cinema").

[7] At the base of all language, at least once originally forgetful humanity has achieved the long-term memory that is a prerequisite of promising (Nietzsche, *On the Genealogy of Morals*), is not communication per se, but promising, thus the idiomatic expressions *be as good as your word* (to keep a promise [*Cambridge International Dictionary of Idioms*]); *give your word* (to promise [*Ibid.*]); *man/woman of your word* (someone who keeps their promises [Ibid.]) (I wonder why we say "I give you my word" but we don't also say: "I give you my image"!). Does "In the beginning was the Word" (John 1:1) also mean "in the beginning was the promise" since to give one's word is to promise? In the beginning God gave his Word, and it was that one day humans will be able to give their word, to promise. Has this promise disappeared with the Nietzschean death of God?

[8] Friedrich Nietzsche, *On the Genealogy of Morals*, trans. Walter Kaufmann and R.J. Hollingdale/*Ecce Homo*, trans. Walter Kaufmann; edited, with commentary, by Walter Kaufmann (New York: Vintage Books, 1989), pp. 57-62. I rearranged the

order of one of the quote's paragraphs.

⁹ More specifically in *al-khayâl al-munfasil*. Ibn al-'Arabî "calls the intermediate world of imagination 'discontiguous imagination' (*al-khayâl al-munfasil*), since it exists independently of the viewer. And he names the soul along with the faculty of imagination 'contiguous imagination' (*al-khayâl al-muttasil*), since these are connected to the viewing subject." (William C. Chittick, *The Sufi Path of Knowledge: Ibn al-'Arabi's Metaphysics of Imagination* [Albany, N.Y.: State University of New York Press, 1989], p. 117). The notion of *khayâl munfasil*, of an imagination independent of the viewer, which we find not only in the Sufism of Ibn al-'Arabî but also in Shi'ite theosophy, will regain currency with the advances in and spread of virtual reality; in Andy and Larry Wachowski's Gnostic film *The Matrix*, 1999, the vast simulation called the Matrix is an example of *khayâl munfasil*, while what each of those within the Matrix, i.e. within the *khayâl munfasil*, subjectively imagines is a *khayâl muttasil*.

¹⁰ Many of those present at the assemblies of 'Âshûrâ' cover their faces with their hands. When they remove their hands one often can see that they were crying. But sometimes, one suddenly espies through a gap between their fingers that they are yawning! In part these yawns are not the effect of boredom at hearing yet again the same stories of the atrocities, but of sleepiness, as these assemblies take place from around 9 p.m. till around midnight. This yawn has the same unsettling effect as the small spot of corruption in the otherwise uncorrupted corpse of a saint: "Ruysbroeck has been buried for five years; he is exhumed; his body is intact and pure (of course—otherwise, there would be no story); *but* 'there was only the tip of the nose which bore a faint but certain trace of corruption.' In the other's perfect and embalmed figure (for that is the degree to which it fascinates me) I perceive suddenly a speck of corruption. This speck is a tiny one: a gesture, a word, an object, a garment, something unexpected which appears (which dawns) from a region I had never even suspected, and suddenly attaches the loved object to a *commonplace* world.… I am *flabbergasted*: I hear a counter-rhythm: something like a syncope in the lovely phrase of the loved being, the noise of a rip in the smooth envelope of the Image" ("The Tip of the Nose," in

Roland Barthes, *A Lover's Discourse: Fragments*, trans. Richard Howard [New York: Hill and Wang, 1978], p. 25). The sleepiness affecting these yawning participants is of the kind that affected the three disciples Jesus Christ selected to accompany him for prayer. He asked them: "Stay here and watch with Me" (Matthew 26:38). He moved *a stone's throw* (Luke 22:41—how incisive is the laconism of this *a stone's throw*) and prayed. Returning to them, he found the three sleeping: "What? Could you not watch with Me one hour?" (Matthew 26:40). Three times does he leave them to pray, each time, upon returning, finding them sleeping. "Are you still sleeping and resting? Behold, the hour is at hand, and the Son of Man is being betrayed…" (Matthew 26:45).

[11] "Respecting the derivation of *insân* [a human being], authors differ (…): the Basrees say that it is from *al-insu* [sociability], and its measure is *fi'lân*; (…) some say that it is from *înâs*, signifiying 'perception,' or 'sight,' and 'knowledge,' and 'sensation' (…) and Mohammad Ibn-'Arafeh El-Wâsitee says that men are called *insiyyûn* because they are seen (*yu'nasûn*, i.e. *yurawn*) and that the jinn are called *jinn* because they are [ordinarily] concealed (*mujtannûn*, i.e. *mutawârûn,*) from the sight of men (…) some (namely, the Koofees, *Misbâh al-Fayyûmî*) say that it is originally *insiyân* (Ibn Barrî, author of the *Annotations on the Sihâh*, with Al-Bustî, *Misbâh al-Fayyûmî, Tâj al-'Arûs,*) of the measure *if'ilân*, from *an-nisyân* ["forgetfulness"], (*al-Misbâh*), and contracted to make it more easy of pronunciation, because of its being so often used." The entry *alif nûn sîn* in Edward William Lane, *An Arabic-English Lexicon*, 8 volumes (Beirut, Lebanon: Librairie du Liban, 1980).

[12] The Great Resurrection of Alamût lasted till 1210.

[13] Friedrich Nietzsche: "I beware of speaking of chemical 'laws': that savours of morality." *The Will to Power*, trans. Walter Kaufmann and R.J. Hollingdale (New York: Random House, 1968), p. 630.

[14] Abdulaziz Abdulhussein Sachedina, *Islamic Messianism: The Idea of the Mahdi in Twelver Shi'ism* (Albany: State University of New York Press, 1981), p. 158.

[15] I find this period so unjust that it seems to me there are, beside the revolutionary one, two exemplary responses to it: a

messianic one and a Gnostic one. The first demands waiting for the messiah ("which is the best of actions during his occultation"), who will in the end fill with justice a world only *transiently* filled with injustice since it is essentially and ultimately good, being created by God, the good God. The second demands the disinvestment from this *demonic* world, which has nothing to do with the good God, but was created by a demiurge.

[16] For example Muhsin al-Amîn: see *Thawrat al-tanzîh: Risâlat al-tanzîh, talîha mawâqif minhâ wa-arâ' fî al-Sayyid Muhsin al-Amîn*, ed. Muhammad al-Qâsim al-Husaynî al-Najafî (Bayrût: Dâr al-Jadîd, 1996).

[17] Many a flagellant's slap against his chest is as sober as the flapping of a bird's wing during flight.

[18] While we should be willing to pay the price for the ability to give promises, and therefore for the memory that is a precondition for promises, should we make sure that promises do not span centuries or millennia, given that the price of such promises is exorbitant?

[19] Jean-Joseph Goux, "Subversion and Consensus: Proletarians, Women, Artists," in *Terror and Consensus: Vicissitudes of French Thought*, ed. Jean-Joseph Goux and Philip R. Wood (Stanford, CA: Stanford University Press, 1998), pp. 37 and 39.

[20] Paul Virilio, *The Information Bomb*, trans. Chris Turner (London: Verso, 2000), pp. 118-119.

[21] 1992 figures; they were 28 hours per week and 23.5 hours per week, respectively, in 1986 (1986 Nielsen Report on Television). According to the Center for Media Education in Washington, DC, watching TV is the #1 after-school activity for 6 to 17 year olds; each year most children spend about 1500 hours in front of the TV and 900 hours in the classroom; and by age 70, most people will have spent about 10 years watching TV.

[22] Jean-Joseph Goux, "Subversion and Consensus: Proletarians, Women, Artists," in *Terror and Consensus: Vicissitudes of French Thought*, ed. Jean-Joseph Goux and Philip R. Wood, p. 39.

[23] Indeed live prematurely in the future through virtual reality using the simulation of extremely powerful computers.

[24] "And when Moses came to Our appointed tryst and his Lord had spoken unto him, he said: My Lord! Show me (Thy Self),

that I may gaze upon Thee. He said: Thou wilt not see Me, but gaze upon the mountain! If it stand still in its place, then thou wilt see Me. And when his Lord revealed (His) glory to the mountain He sent it crashing down" (Qur'ân 7:143, trans. Pickthall).

[25] There are two sorts of people I distrust and with whom I feel no affinity whatsoever: those who acquiesce to low interpretations and those who artificially, without rigor and honesty, pushed by no necessity emanating from them or the object, try to enrich the object, in the process cheapening the act of enriching itself.

[26] Edward William Lane, *An Arabic-English Lexicon*, entry *shîn hâ' dâl*.

[27] *The American Heritage Talking Dictionary*.

[28] I have already posed the question whether all humans are mortal in the strong sense in my book *Forthcoming* (2000), where I wrote in the section "Oedipus in Egypt": "Endless death is so exemplarily embodied in the ancient Egyptian anthropoid coffins, sculptures, and reliefs, that I almost find it impossible to believe what I know: the diminutive people walking around in the Egyptian Museum of Antiquities—obviously I include myself among them—are themselves always already dead; and that I almost believe, as did the Egyptians of the Ancient Kingdom, that death is the prerogative of only the few, and that the people walking around in the museum are wholly within life… that they encounter death only as an external event…." I elaborated in the footnote: "Is it possible that indeed only a few die? To die, to be an undead, is already a form of courage: owing to over-turns in the undeath realm, even turning back is forging ahead. (Un)death is not for cowards. Cowardice applies only in situations from which one can escape; there is no cowardice past the point of no-return. A coward can enter or find himself or herself neither in a labyrinth, nor in undeath, nor in the orthodox Christian or Moslem hell—he or she can find himself or herself in the hell concocted by mind-projections in the bardo of becoming, since he or she can escape from the latter by rebirth… If we rather discover that we all die, that is become undead, then that would mean that we are all fundamentally courageous."

²⁹ Al-imâm an-Nawawî, *Gardens of the Righteous*.

³⁰ *Sahîh al-Bukhârî*, 2ⁿᵈ ed., no. 3887 (Beirut, Lebanon: Dâr al-Kutub al-'ilmiyya, 2002); cf. *The Encyclopaedia of Islam*, new ed., volume VII, entry *Mi'râdj* (Leiden: Brill, 1993), p. 98 for another account: "When they [Gabriel, Michael and a third angel] found him [the Prophet] sleeping, they laid him on his back, opened his body, brought water from the Zamzam well and washed away all that they found within his body of doubt, idolatry, paganism and error. They then brought a golden vessel which was filled with wisdom and belief. Thereupon he was taken up to the lowest heaven."

³¹ Contrariwise, for Leibniz, "what we call death is envelopment and diminution" (*Monadology* 73); cf. Deleuze's 29 April 1980 Vincennes lecture on Leibniz: "In other words, death is nothing other than an envelopment; perceptions cease being developed into conscious perceptions, they are enveloped in an infinity of minute perceptions. Or yet again, he [Leibniz] says, [death is] sleep without dreaming in which there are lots of minute perceptions."

³² Tabarî, *The History of al-Tabarî* (*Ta'rîkh al-rusul wa'l-mulûk*), vol. IX, *The Last Years of the Prophet*, translated and annotated by Ismail K. Poonawala (Albany: State University of New York Press, 1990), p. 185.

³³ From a poem written by 'Alî Zayn al-'Âbidîn (d. 95/714), the fourth Shi'ite Imâm, a survivor of the massacre of much of the family and many of the companions of the prophet Muhammad at Karbalâ': "I conceal the jewels of my knowledge—For fear that some ignorant man, on seeing the truth, should crush us… O Lord! If I were to reveal one pearl of my gnosis—They would say to me: are you then a worshipper of idols?—And there would be Muslims who would see justice in the shedding of my blood!—They find abominable the most beautiful thing they are offered" (quoted in Henry Corbin, *History of Islamic Philosophy*, trans. Liadain Sherrard with the assistance of Philip Sherrard [London; New York: Kegan Paul International, 1993], p. 38).

³⁴ From Ibn Bâkûyâ's *Hallaj's Life as Recounted by His Son Hamd* (the only memorial excluded from the transmission ban decreed in 922 and enforced till the end of the 'Abbasid Caliphate), quoted in Louis Massignon, *The Passion of al-Hallâj*:

Mystic and Martyr of Islam, trans. Herbert Mason, vol. 1 (Princeton: Princeton University Press, 1982), pp. 16-18. The act of giving witness can be so unbearable to watch or even to hear or read about that it breaks the receiver's sensory-motor link, turning him or her into a witness, a martyr. Did this happen to one or more of those who witnessed Hallâj's ordeal on the gibbet or even heard about it? Yes, it happened at least to his disciple Shakir, who returned from Khurasân to Baghdâd, where his master was excommunicated and executed, only to be himself executed there.

[35] *The Travels of Marco Polo*, introduction by John Masefield (London: J.M. Dent & sons; New York: E.P. Dutton & co., 1954), pp. 74-76.

[36] See Farhad Daftary, *The Assassin Legends: Myths of the Isma'ilis*. London; New York: I.B. Tauris, 2001.

[37] Muqtadâ al-Sadr has had the degrading hubris of calling the slovenly, badly trained militia he assembled "The Army of the Mahdî." It is to the dishonor of contemporary Usûlî Twelver Shi'ites that such a demeaning misnaming was not condemned outright. Establishing the army of the Mahdî during the latter's occultation, when in principle it should be contemporaneous with his appearance, is a way of *forcing the* [messianic] *end*, and that has, as in Judaism, to be censored. Unlike Nizârî Ismâ'îlism of the era of the Great Resurrection (*al-qiyâma al-kubra*), which performed the immediate worldly enactment of the Resurrection, and which exemplifies within the context of Islam the second of Messianism's two paradigmatic tendencies, Twelver Shi'ism's main task in the worldly absence of the Mahdî is to take to the limit the experience of and thinking about waiting and the promise (why was it not a Twelver Shi'ite or a Jew who came up with *Waiting for Godot?*). Therefore, anything that tends to weaken waiting and the promise, such as *wilâyat al faqîh* (governance by the jurisprudent), implemented by Khumaynî in Iran, undermines one of the main reasons of the continued existence of this sect. Past the Lesser Occultation, during which the twelfth imâm still conveyed his instructions to his followers through his four consecutive special representatives, in principle the following prerogatives of the twelfth imâm have been, since his Greater Occultation, in abeyance until his return: proclaiming and leading the Holy War (*jihâd*)—thus shaykh Ja'far Kâshifu-l-Ghitâ's *fatwâ* (legal

decision) of Holy War against the Russians during the first Russo-Iranian war (1804-1813) is illegitimate; leading the congregational Friday prayer; administering the Qur'ânic legal punishments (*hudûd*); and receiving the religious taxes of *zakât* and *khums* ("One Fifth," a twenty per cent tax on a Shi'ite's excess annual profits)—at least the half of the *khums* due to him—as well as the land tax (*kharâj*). I disagree with the delegation of these functions to the 'ulamâ' as the self-appointed "general representative" (*nâ'ib 'âmm*) of the imâm, considering it a usurpation of his prerogatives. Even more than the ignorance and bad training of Muqtadâ al-Sadr's armed followers, what made Muqtadâ al-Sadr's misnaming his militia "The Army of the Mahdî" the epitome of the derisory is how frequently he and his spokesmen reneged on their agreements with others, repeatedly breaking their promises, including concerning evacuating the shrine of imâm 'Alî in Najaf, which his militia had desecrated by making it a military base. Here's a nightmarishly derisory messianic scenario that befits Muqtadâ al-Sadr and his rabble: a Mahdî who keeps his word, reappearing on the Earth notwithstanding the passage of over a millennium since his Greater Occultation, only then to break a new promise over an insignificant matter! This would add another paradoxical and stupefying kind of messiah to the three ones I listed in my book *Undying Love, or Love Dies* (Post-Apollo Press, 2002): a crucified messiah (Jesus Christ); an apostate one (Sabbatai Zevi, *alias* Mehemed Kapici Bashi); and an Antichrist, a messiah in hell ("Jesus said, 'Whoever is near me is near the fire, and whoever is far from me is far from the kingdom'" [*The Gospel of Thomas* #82]) "to show that hell, which is not a locus of suffering for debased humans but the unbearable suffering of being banished away from God, can be endured (at the highest spiritual level), and thus spare Iblîs succumbing to the temptation of trying to forget, and consequently do away with the need for the continuing existence of the debased states as a manner of forgetting the disaster of being banished away from the Beloved, God."

[38] See Nir Rosen, "Shiite Contender Eyes Iraq's Big Prize," *Time*, Saturday, 3 May 2003; and Rory McCarthy, "Shia gunmen clash with US troops," *The Guardian*, 8 May 2004.

[39] On returning from one of his military expeditions, the messenger of God Muhammad said to his companions: "We have

returned from *al-jihâd al-asghar* (the Lesser Holy War) to *al-jihâd al-akbar* (the Greater Holy War)." Some companions asked: "What is the Greater Holy War, O Messenger of God?" He replied: "The Holy War against the *nafs* ('those attributes of the servant that are infirm' [Ibn al-'Arabî, *Istilâhât al-sûfiyya*])." Have not many Sûfîs waged such a Holy War (against the thoughts from the devil and from the self)? And have not many of them died (before dying physically) in the way of God while engaged in this Holy War, enduring *fanâ'* (obliteration in God)? And is it not the case that with many of them, one should not call them dead, but alive, since they have acceded to *baqâ'* (subsistence in God)? Since only a prophet or a messenger of God, who is in charge mainly and exoterically of the exoteric (esoterically, each messenger [*rasûl*] of God, who receives through an Angel a new law [*sharî'a*], which he proclaims, inaugurating a new religious period, is also an imâm), can legitimately lead into the Lesser Holy War some of his followers who had not already fully engaged in the Greater Holy War, thus who have not already achieved the removal of the cover and therefore who are not yet truly alive, were a Twelver Shi'ite imâm or a Sûfî shaykh, who are in charge of *ta'wîl*, i.e. of carrying the exoteric sense of the religious law back to its esoteric sense, thus of removing the cover, to do so, they are bound to be viewed by some of their followers as prophets or messengers of God. This happened in the case of 'Alî b. Abî Tâlib, the fourth caliph and the first Shi'ite imâm, who was viewed by some Shi'ite so-called extremist sects (*ghulât*) as a prophet. Were the nine Twelver Shi'ite imâms who came after slaughtered imâm Husayn "quietists," or were it rather the case that, being in charge of the esoteric sense, they knew that their followers must engage in the Lesser Holy War only after engaging successfully in the Greater Holy War, i.e. only after they have achieved the removal of the cover and became truly alive? While a number of Twelver Shi'ite traditions and reports indicate, when read exoterically, that the long-dead previous imâms, who according to Twelver Shi'ites were all treacherously killed (by poisoning…), will return along with their long-dead supporters during the reappearance of the Mahdî to take revenge on their enemies, who will also be resurrected for that reason; I believe that, read esoterically, these traditions about such a return (*raj'a*) intimate that these imâms and their supporters had seen with a piercing sight and are therefore still alive and will be still alive when the Mahdî reappears. They, along with all those who are truly alive, paradigmatically "the resurrection and the life," Jesus Christ, will be part of the Army of the Mahdî. I wager that al-Hallâj will be one of them, while his contemporary Twelver Shi'ite accusers will not. The Mahdî's army will consist of martyrs. Of all of Muqtadâ al-Sadr's followers who died during the pointless insurrections he led, *none* will return and be a member of the Army of the Mahdî during the latter's reappearance.

[40] Cf. Jeremiah 5:21 and Ezekiel 12:2.

[41] The latter can only be bought and sold by others, as in the case of the ancient tribal custom of the payment of *blood money* to settle disputes and end feuds (this custom is still practiced in rural areas in Egypt and it is, unfortunately, regaining currency in presently regressed Iraq); or else stolen, at both its beginning and its end: Artaud, "Now, the hideous history of the Demiurge / is well known / It is the history of the body / … which, in order to go first and be born, / projected itself across my body / and / was born / through the disemboweling of my body / of which he kept a piece / in order to / pass himself off / as me.…" and "besides, one does not commit suicide by oneself. / No one has ever been born by oneself. / No one dies by oneself either. / … And I believe that there is always someone else, at the extreme moment of death, to strip us of our own life" (*Van Gogh, the Man Suicided by Society*, 1947). Was the death of Jesus Christ, who twice predicted it, the second time on his way to Jerusalem, saying to his twelve disciples, "the Son of Man will be betrayed to the chief priests and the teachers of the law. They will condemn him to death and will turn him over to the Gentiles to be mocked and flogged and crucified" (Matthew 20: 17-19); and that of al-Hallâj, who told the people gathered at the Mansûr Mosque, "'Know that God most high has made my blood licit for you, so kill me.… Kill me, you will be rewarded, and I will find rest,'" then said to the reporter of this tradition: "There is no duty in the world more important for Muslims than killing me," and then recited, "Between me and You [God] there's an 'I am' that's crowding me. Ah! Remove with Your 'I am' my 'I am' from between us," purloined from them? Were both actually crucified? Or was it the case that, for the protracted duration of the Passion, it was another

who was substituted for each of the two? When "the Muʻtazilite Abû'l-Hâshim Balkhî came to insult him [Husayn ibn Mansûr al-Hallâj on the gibbet]: 'Praise be to God, Who has put you on view there, an example to men and to angels, as a warning for spectators' … he felt Husayn himself behind him, his hand was resting on his shoulder blade and he was reciting the verse (Qur'ân 4: 156): 'no they (the Jews: here the Muslims) did not kill him (Christ: here Hallâj) and they did not crucify him; rather they were deluded (*shubbiha lahum*: by a *sosia*?)'" (Louis Massignon, *The Passion of al-Hallâj: Mystic and Martyr of Islam*, vol. 1, p. 595. How fitting that on Hallâj's way from prison to the esplanade where he was to be executed, "the crowd formed into a mob; the commissioner, afraid of being killed [or: lest someone kill Hallâj] said: 'this is not he, Hallâj; Hallâj is still in the *Dâr al-Wazîr* [the vizir's mansion]')" [from the Official Testimony of the Clerk of Court, Zanjî, quoted in Ibid., p. 569]). If someone else was substituted for Jesus Christ during the Passion, this would be either because God responded affirmatively to His Son's imploration: "Father, if you are willing, take this cup from me; yet not my will, but yours be done" (Luke 22:42); or else because someone managed to rob Jesus of his crucifixion and die in place of the one who had come to die in place of humans. Had not Jesus Christ himself intimated an uncanny structural correspondence between the thief and the Son of Man when he said: "If the owner of the house had known at what hour the thief was coming, he would not have let his house be broken into. You also must be ready, because the Son of Man will come at an hour when you do not expect him" (Luke 12: 39-40)?! If there was a substitution, it must have taken place by the time the accused who was brought before the Sanhedrin said: "But *from now on*, the Son of Man will be seated at the right hand of the mighty God" (Luke 22:69, my italics). Was this partly why the Apostle Peter denied thrice that he knows him? And if Peter sensed that the accused was not the Christ, it must be through the same kind of revelation that had allowed him earlier to answer Jesus' question to his disciples, "Who do you say I am?" with: "You are the Christ, the Son of the living God"—Jesus replied, "Blessed are you, Simon son of Jonah, for this was not revealed to you by man, but by my Father in heaven" (Matthew 16: 15-17). But how would the other onlookers have been able to discern whether they were in the presence of the Son of Man or an imposter if "no one knows who the Son is except the Father" (Luke 10:22)? If he did not respond to the passers by who hurled insults at him, shaking their heads and saying, "You who are going to destroy the temple and build it in three days, save yourself! Come down from the cross, if you are the Son of God!" (Matthew 27:39-40), it was possibly not because his crucifixion was part of the divine plan, but because the one who was crucified with the written notice "This is Jesus, The King of the Jews" above his head was not the Son of God, but either a substitute or an impostor. In which case it is fitting that two robbers were crucified alongside him. In case he was a substitute, these words said on the cross take on quite a different meaning: "Father, forgive them, for they do not know what they are doing" (Luke 23:34; some early manuscripts do not have this sentence). In case the one who was crucified was an imposter, it is possible that this imposter was none other than the antichrist—the one who, among other things, *steals the name* "Christ" (there is always an imposter to try to usurp witnessing and martyrdom, an anti-witness, an anti-martyr: in the case of al-Hallâj, the eighty-four cosigners of the *mahdar* of condemnation, called the "upright witnesses" (*shuhûd 'udûl*), who were present at the execution in order to hear and repeat the judge's standard "his blood on my neck," thus jointly taking responsibility for the carrying out of the sentence). At the onset of his psychosis, of his dying before his physical death, Nietzsche, the author of *The Antichrist* (September 1888), signed with *The Crucified* his missives to August Strindberg (early January 1889), Meta von Salis (3 January 1889), Georg Brandes (4 January), Heinrich Koselitz (5 January), Malwida von Meysenbug (around 4 January), "the illustrious Polonese" (around 4 January), Cardinal Mariani (around 4 January), and Umberto I, King of Italy (around 4 January). There would be no contradiction between the title of his book and his signature if the one who was crucified was not the Christ but possibly the antichrist. And if the one who was crucified was a substitute, might this substitute not have been, across chronological time, a certain Friedrich Nietzsche?

[42] One of the greatest *lines of flight* is *al-hijra*, the migration of the prophet Muhammad and his followers from Mecca, his native town, to Yathrib (subsequently renamed *madînat al-nabî* [the city of the Prophet], for short: Madîna) in 622, thenceforth year 1 of the Muslim calendar.

[43] Tabarî, *The History of al-Tabarî*, vol. IX, *The Last Years of the Prophet*, p. 185. Is 'Umar b. al-Khattâb right or wrong in proclaiming this? If the prophet Muhammad is infallible (*ma'sûm*), then he cannot die since to die is to be guilty, thus fallible, if not for any specific act then for feeling guilty as such.

[44] See *The Encyclopaedia of Islam*, new ed., volume II, entry *ghulât* (Leiden: Brill, 1965), p. 1094; and Muhammad Ben 'abd Al-Karîm Al-Shahrastânî, *Kitâb al-milal: les dissidences de l'islam*, presentation and traduction par Jean-Claude Vadet (Paris: Librairie Orientaliste Paul Geuthner, 1984), p. 292.

[45] Who but a great visionary who has healed many a blind man would behave in the following manner: "Jesus saw a person committing theft. Jesus asked, 'Did you commit theft?' The man answered, 'Never! I swear by Him than whom there is none worthier of worship.' Jesus said, 'I believe God and falsify my eye.'" (Hammâm ibn Munabbih, *Sahîfat Hammâm ibn Munabbih*, no. 41, quoted in *The Muslim Jesus: Sayings and Stories in Islamic Literature*, ed. and trans. Tarif Khalidi [Cambridge, MA: Harvard University Press, 2001], p. 51; Cf. *Sahîh al-Bukhârî*, 2nd ed., no. 3444 [Beirut, Lebanon: Dâr al-Kutub al-'ilmiyya, 2002])? Cf. Ludwig Wittgenstein: "If a blind man were to ask me 'Have you got two hands?' I should not make sure by looking. If I were to have any doubt of it, then I don't know why I should trust my eyes. For why shouldn't I test my *eyes* by looking to find out whether I see my two hands? What is to be tested by what? (Who decides what stands fast?)" (*On Certainty*, ed. G. E. M. Anscombe and G. H. von Wright; trans. Denis Paul and G. E. M. Anscombe [Oxford: Basil Blackwell, 1979], #125).

[46] It is amazing that there was no outcry from those Muslims who sued Youssef Chahine over his weak kitschy film *The Emigrant*, 1994, whose protagonist is modeled on the prophet Joseph, concerning Mel Gibson's excruciating film *The Passion of the Christ* (2004) about one of the main prophets of Islam.

[47] From the Official Testimony of the Clerk of Court, Zanjî, quoted in Louis Massignon, *The Passion of al-Hallâj: Mystic and Martyr of Islam*, vol. 1, p. 571.

[48] Ibid., p. 624.

⁴⁹ On the break of the sensory-motor link, see Chapter 1 of Gilles Deleuze's *Cinema 2: The Time-Image*, trans. Hugh Tomlinson and Robert Galeta (Minneapolis: University of Minnesota Press, 1986).

⁵⁰ The one really beautiful shot in Mel Gibson's excruciating *The Passion of the Christ*, 2004, occurs in the film's last scene: suddenly, the crucified Christ is filmed from a heavenly perspective, with the sort of detachment, colors, rocks, haze, and, most importantly, ("third fullness, two-thirds") emptiness that one encounters most characteristically in traditional Chinese painting, so that we move from a Semitic to a Chinese atmosphere and culture. It would seem that high up, there is no God but a sort of Taoist Way of Heaven.

⁵¹ François Cheng, *Empty and Full: The Language of Chinese Painting*, trans. Michael H. Kohn (Boston: Shambhala, 1994), pp. 76-77.

⁵² Actually in 213 BC, in the China of Shih huang-ti, "all books not dealing with agriculture, medicine, or prognostication were burned, except historical records of Ch'in and books in the imperial library" (*Encyclopedia Britannica*).

⁵³ Jorge Luis Borges, *The Total Library: Non-Fiction 1922-1986*, ed. Eliot Weinberger; trans. Esther Allen, Suzanne Jill Levine and Eliot Weinberger (London; New York: Penguin, 2001), pp. 344-345.

⁵⁴ "A functional electronic nano-device has been manufactured using biological self-assembly for the first time.... A team of Israeli scientists [at the Technion-Israel Institute of Technology] harnessed the construction capabilities of DNA and the electronic properties of carbon nanotubes to create the self-assembling nano-transistor." *New Scientist*, 20 November 2003.

⁵⁵ Jorge Luis Borges, *The Total Library: Non-Fiction 1922-1986*, p. 345.

⁵⁶ I encourage the readers of this book to sign the online petition "Stop the Wall Immediately" initiated by French philosopher Etienne Balibar: http://www.petitiononline.com/stw/petition.html

⁵⁷ The unbearable can be borne by a Muslim not by committing a veiled suicide, which is prohibited in Islam and which anyway will lead him or her to death where one has piercing sight, but by reaching a stage of *fanâ'* (obliteration in God), in

which it is God who is "his sight through which he sees," and God, Who created the universe in which such a thing can occur, can certainly bear it.

It is only God (the Father) Who, in his infinite compassion, magnanimity, etc., can withstand to be insulted, tortured and then crucified (in the person of the Son). A (great) human should not be able to withstand that this should happen to God. The ordeal on the cross could have lasted much longer, indeed until the end of the world, had not Jesus of Nazareth succumbed, and he succumbed so quickly not because of the torture he suffered and the flagellation and the crucifixion, but from not being able to tolerate that (the Son of) God, who had incarnated in him, should be treated thus by low-lives (it is reported that on viewing an advanced screening of Mel Gibson's *The Passion of the Christ* [2004], the Pope said: "It is as it was"; I would like to believe that he meant by that not that Gibson's film shows the events as they happened then, but that the film itself is a reenactment, by a low-life, of the torture and crucifixion of Christ). It is with the resurrection that Jesus partook of God. Had they tried to crucify the resurrected body of Jesus Christ, then he would not have succumbed until the end of the world. So along with being the becoming human of God (Jesus Christ), Christianity could not but be the becoming God of men and women so that they would not perish from considering what happened to God on the cross.

In films dealing with monotheistic religions, the filmmaker has no right, unless he wants to assume the status of God, to film the events from an "objective" point of view, but has to show the events from the subjective points of view of various "historical" witnesses, with the consequence that he will end up showing only certain parts of what happened, a fragmentary rendering. For a filmmaker to narrate his film's events from a perspective that is both omnipresent (through parallel montage) and omniscient is to implicitly assume the point of view of God. We see this explicitly and naively in Mel Gibson's *The Passion of the Christ* in a symptomatic shot in the scene of the crucifixion: when Jesus gives up his spirit, the scene is suddenly filmed from a heavenly perspective, from God's view. A filmmaker can legitimately do so only if he has progressed so far on the spiritual path as to have attained the mystical station of obliteration in God (the Sûfîs' *fanâ'*), for then his camera shows events from the perspective of God not because the filmmaker knows what God is seeing but because he is absent and God has become "his hearing through which he hears, his sight through which he sees" ("My servant draws near to Me through nothing I love more than that which I have made obligatory for him. My servant never ceases drawing near to Me through supererogatory works until I love him. Then, when I love him, I am his hearing through which he hears, his sight through which he sees, his hand through which he grasps, and his foot through which he walks" [a *hadîth qudsî*]).

[58] The statement "I am the *shahîd(a)* [martyr] (name of speaker)," with which, starting with the Lebanese Sanâ' Yûsif Muhaydlî, a number of guerrilla fighters introduced their prerecorded video testimonies, is paradoxical whether said by a secular person or by a Muslim. For when a secular resistance fighter, for instance a communist, says it, he or she is telling us that he or she is dead! (See my essay "I Am the Martyr Sanâ' Yûsif Muhaydlî" in the revised and expanded edition of my book *(Vampires): An Uneasy Essay on the Undead in Film* [Sausalito, CA: The Post-Apollo Press, 2003]). And when a Muslim resistance fighter says it, he or she is telling us that past the bombing operation in which he or she died physically he or she is a living witness!

[59] If martyrdom, whether secular or Islamic, is related to death, it is because being a witness, the primary sense of both *martyr* and *shahîd*, is related to death: Islamic martyrdom is related to death because it is through death that one has piercing sight; and secular martyrdom is related to death because it is through some sort of breakdown of the sensory-motor link that one has a visionary view of reality, which vision may in unfortunate cases be so unbearable that the one who undergoes it attempts or at least entertains suicide.

[60] In the first half of 2005, at least 213 suicide attacks—172 by vehicle and 41 by bombers on foot—took place in Iraq, according to an Associated Press count. It is estimated that less than 10% of the more than 500 suicide attacks that have taken place in Iraq since 2003 have been carried out by Iraqis.

Jalal Toufic is a writer, film theorist, and video artist. He is the author of *Distracted* (Station Hill, 1991; 2nd ed., Tuumba, 2003), *(Vampires): An Uneasy Essay on the Undead in Film* (Station Hill, 1993; 2nd ed., Post-Apollo, 2003), *Over-Sensitivity* (Sun & Moon, 1996), *Forthcoming* (Atelos, 2000), *Undying Love, or Love Dies* (Post-Apollo, 2002), and *Two or Three Things I'm Dying to Tell You* (Post-Apollo, 2005). His videos and mixed-media works, which include *Credits Included: A Video in Red and Green* (1995), *Radical Closure Artist with Bandaged Sense Organ* (1997), *Overlooking the Unsightly to See* (2000), *The Sleep of Reason: This Blood Spilled in My Veins* (2002), *'Âshûrâ': This Blood Spilled in My Veins* (2002), *Saving Face* (2003), *I Am the Martyr Comrade Jamâl Sâtî* (2003), *This Is Not to Say that This Is Not the Case* (2004), *A Special Effect Termed "Time"; or, Filming Death at Work* (2005), and *The Lamentations Series: The Ninth Night and Day* (2005), have been presented in New York (Artists Space); San Francisco (the San Francisco Cinematheque, the Lab and Yerba Buena Center for the Arts); Berkeley (Pacific Film Archive); Los Angeles (UCLA Film and TV Archive); Barcelona (Fundació Antoni Tàpies); Rotterdam (Witte de With); Brussels (Palais des Beaux-Arts); London (London International Festival of Theatre); Berlin (House of World Cultures and BüroFriedrich); Munich (Galerie Tanit); Toronto (YYZ Artists' Outlet); Marseille (centre international de poésie); Athens (the National Museum of Contemporary Art); Sao Paulo (Videobrasil); Umeå, Sweden (BildMuseet); Prague (FUTURA Centre for Contemporary Art); Bologna (Arte Fiera); Cairo (Townhouse Gallery); Jerusalem (Al-Ma'mal Foundation for Contemporary Art and Khalil Sakakini Cultural Centre Foundation); Beirut; and most recently at the 16th International Documentary Filmfestival Amsterdam (IDFA) in a "Focus Jalal Toufic" program. He co-edited the special *Discourse* issue *Gilles Deleuze: A Reason to Believe in this World*, and edited the special *Discourse* issues *Middle Eastern Films Before Thy Gaze Returns to Thee* and *Mortals to Death* as well as the *Review of Photographic Memory* (Arab Image Foundation, 2004). Toufic has taught at the University of California at Berkeley, California Institute of the Arts, USC, San Francisco State University, and, in Amsterdam, DasArts and the Rijksakademie. He is currently the Head of the MA program in Film/Video Studies at Holy Spirit University, Lebanon. Website: http://www.jalaltoufic.com.